D1631171

D

# Nellie's Book

## The Early Life of
## Victoria Wood's Mother

CHRIS FOOTE WOOD

FOREWORD BY
Victoria Wood

SUTTON PUBLISHING

First published in 2006 by
Sutton Publishing Limited · Phoenix Mill
Thrupp · Stroud · Gloucestershire · GL5 2BU

British Library Cataloguing in Publication Data
A catalogue record for this book is available from the British Library.

ISBN 0-7509-4180-4

Typeset in 11/14pt Garamond.
Typesetting and origination by
Sutton Publishing Limited.
Printed and bound in England by
J.H. Haynes & Co. Ltd, Sparkford.

# Contents

# Foreword

## *by* Victoria Wood

When my brother Chris told me he was going to write a book based on our mother's early life, I was happy for him to go ahead, as long as I didn't have to do anything! My mother was a very intelligent and forceful person, very academically able, a natural writer. I always felt she had been born out of her time, that the role of housewife and stay-at-home mother was a huge frustration to her – she put herself through college and university in her forties, starting as soon as I, the youngest, was in secondary school. I think now she should have done this much earlier and not bothered bringing me up at all!

She didn't talk much about her early life – I knew she was a Rechabite, a lifelong teetotaller, that she was brought up in quite poor circumstances in the Bradford district of Manchester, that she had been a Young Communist, and had done some work with Joan Littlewood during the war. Most of the time, however, she was too busy to chat, driving around Lancashire in her Austin van, liberating bits of spare timber from building sites to use for bookshelves, or screeching to a halt outside junk shops, eager to acquire yet more chairs, or books, or old theatrical costumes, or, once, a sack of shoe lasts.

Our house, a children's holiday home on the moors above the Rossendale Valley, was crammed with stuff – you had to move along the corridors sideways, and when our father died, and mother moved to a bungalow, it was a huge job to clear it all out. I will never forget arriving to help my sisters and seeing them standing helplessly in the kitchen looking at an array of at least fourteen old Thermoses, some still holding soup.

Her last few years were spent bedridden in her bungalow, but even then she managed to acquire yet more stuff. How a woman who couldn't even walk managed to fill her garage with wardrobes which were in turn filled with damp Victorian novels remains a baffler.

I did a lot of the junk clearing, but didn't want to keep many of my mother's possessions. I can't bear hoarding and didn't have the time or the spare energy to sort through all her papers and mementos. Chris took on this job and, from what mother left of her writings, has put together her story – her childhood as one of six children in a poor family in Manchester in the twenties and thirties. I hope you enjoy it.

# Acknowledgements

So many people have helped me with this book, it is simply not possible to list them all. First and foremost there is of course my mother Helen Colleen (Nellie). Not only did she bring me into the world, she also left me her original manuscript of 'Empire Street' and enough material from her and my father Stan for several books. I am grateful to my three sisters, Penelope, Rosalind and Victoria, for their support, and particularly to Victoria for her contribution. Without them, this book would not have been written.

In my researches, I have been greatly helped and encouraged by Fr Tim Hopkins and members of the combined parish of St Anne's, St Brigid's, St Michael and St Vincent in Manchester; Manchester Libraries; Manchester City Art Galleries; the *Manchester Evening News*; the Rechabite Friendly Society; the Costume Society; the National Monuments Record; and the Ordnance Survey. Special thanks go to the Manchester and Lancashire Family History Society. It has been a joy to explore their wonderful archive, and the friendly MLFHS members and voluntary workers could not have been more helpful. My uncle Bernard, Aunties Muriel, Jean and Irene, and cousins Maureen, Bernadette and Susan, have all helped with their reminiscences and photographs. My nephew, Madza Hewitt, helped to sort out the family collection. Being strictly a 'two-finger' typist, I have had a good deal of secretarial help. Particular thanks go to Beryl Pratt for transcribing my mother's original notes, and to Debra Atkinson for her audio-typing.

My grateful thanks also go to my agent, Robert Dudley, and Sutton Publishing for putting their faith in a first-time author, despite the fact that he was well past sixty. My editors, Sarah Bryce, Sarah Flight and Clare Jackson at Sutton Publishing, have been most kind and patient.

No words can express the deep gratitude and love I feel for my dear wife Frances Foote. I changed my name from Wood to Foote Wood when we married in 1977. Returning to paid employment after twenty-four years of dedicated and unpaid voluntary work, this wonderful woman readily agreed to help me in my ambition to become a full-time writer by supporting me financially and in every other way possible. Without Frances's generous sacrifice and her unshakeable faith in me, this, the start of my third career, would not have been possible.

Chris Foote Wood
Bishop Auckland

# Introduction

## When Nellie Met Stan

Nellie Mape met Stanley Wood at 4.30 p.m. on Boxing Day, 26 December 1937. She was just eighteen, a politically active Lancashire factory lass with dreams of romantic love. He was twenty-five, an insurance claims inspector turned part-time musician and freelance journalist with ambitions to be a successful author. Their union produced one of the most remarkable talents of our time, the hugely popular and much-loved comic performer, writer, singer, actress, producer and 'national treasure' Victoria Wood. Victoria, born in 1953, is the youngest of Stan and Nellie's four children. She follows Christopher (me, born 1940), Penelope (1945) and Rosalind (1950).

Nellie and Stan were both born and brought up in Manchester, but on the other hand they could hardly have been more different in their backgrounds, character and temperament. Nellie came from a large and impoverished Irish Catholic, working-class family for whom getting by was a daily struggle. Stan was the only child of a genteel, lower-middle class couple who were comfortably off by the standards of the day.

Nellie's mother Ada worked at the cotton mill across the street to keep the family afloat. Her husband Jack, unable to work due to poor health, looked after Nellie as a child until she was old enough to go to nursery school. Stan was spoiled rotten by his mother Eleanor. She did not work and was able to indulge in her favourite pastimes of golf, bridge and cocktails, thanks to her husband John having a secure job in the telegraphy department at Manchester Post Office.

As well as working at Marsland's cotton-spinning mill, Ada indefatigably kept house for her husband and their six surviving children (two died young) in their tiny, rented two-up two-down terraced house, cheek by jowl with mills, factories, chemical and dye works, and even an adjacent abattoir, by the canal in industrial East Manchester.

Eleanor was an unenthusiastic housewife and a poor cook. In her youth, the servants had done all that! Eleanor had two immediate priorities on marrying John (who would later win the Croix de Guerre in the First World War) in 1911: firstly, to have no more children – Stan was already on the way – and, secondly, to move from Moss Side to their own semi-detached house with garden back and front in the leafy South Manchester suburb of Chorlton-cum-Hardy. Naturally, her Stanley had to go to a good school and get a good job.

Nellie went to the local Catholic Girls' School. Despite being almost always top of her class, she missed out on the scholarship exams and left school for a job as a progress-chaser at the nearby steelworks days after her fourteenth birthday. Having started her schooling a year earlier than most of her contemporaries, Nellie had two years in the top class. She always had the tag of being the youngest and the bossiest in her form. Invariably taking the lead in street games and childhood expeditions to the local park and beyond, Nellie made up and acted out her own stories – 'soap operas', she called them – for her playmates and classmates. In her final year at school, she helped to teach the 'Dunces', but was denied the position of head girl by the headmistress, despite being recommended for it by her form teacher.

Nellie argued with her teachers and defied them. She continued her membership of the Juvenile Rechabites (the popular temperance movement), despite being instructed by her head teacher to leave this non-Catholic organisation. Nellie continued to read *Jane Eyre* in defiance of her class teacher, who condemned it as an immoral book. The 'little fat girl', as her teacher once called her, was close to her father as a youngster, but later Nellie argued with him and defied him too. When Jack Mape gave his wilful teenage daughter the ultimatum that she was to stop going to political meetings and rallies (Nellie was by then a keen member of the Young Communist League) or he would throw her out of the house, Nellie did not hesitate. She promptly left home to live with another single girl workmate, a hugely brave decision at her age and in that era. One version of this story is that Jack physically threw Nellie out of the house, into the cold, the dark and the rain, in her stockinged feet and without a coat or hat. The younger children ran upstairs and threw Nellie's hat, coat and shoes to her out of the bedroom window.

Stan was a gifted musician and writer. He played piano in a large dance orchestra in Manchester, in his own smaller dance band, and in jazz groups. He wrote songs and arranged music while working as an insurance claims inspector before going full-time as a musician and freelance journalist. Serving in the Royal Navy during the Second World War, Lieutenant Stanley Wood wrote, organized and ran hugely successful shows and reviews. He edited the Navy magazine *Guzz*.

Before the war, Stan had written humorous articles for several motorcycling and car magazines. While still in his teens, he wrote and produced sketches and short plays for his local dramatic society. In 1947, Stan had his first novel *Death on a Smokeboat* published under his pen name Ross Graham, but after that his main written output was for radio. As well as factual and historical items, Stan had great success with his radio plays and sketches. He wrote gags for Wilfred Pickles, the actor and radio personality. Later, Stan became a scriptwriter for the seminal television soap *Coronation Street*. His stage musical *Clogs!* was a provincial success. He wrote songs, too.

Having grown up through the twenties and thirties with millions suffering real hunger and unemployment, and with a growing family to feed, clothe and educate, Stan never gave up his day job to write full-time – even though he kept promising himself he would. After earning a modest and precarious living as Liberal parliamentary agent for the Bury & Radcliffe constituency from 1946 to 1950, Stan returned to insurance while remaining active in the Liberal Party. For the rest of his life he worked for the Manufacturers Life of Canada, being one of their most successful agents in the UK, while still writing prolifically. Stan kept on working until shortly before his death at the age of eighty-one.

Nellie worked too, as determined as Stan was to give their children the best possible start in life. During the war she worked for comedian Arthur Askey, and also as a barmaid and a civil servant. After the war she worked as a telephonist and then part-time as a market researcher. Returning to education in later life as a mature student, Nellie made up for lost time by gaining BA and MA degrees at Manchester University. She became a lecturer at Bolton Technical College and also an examiner. Nellie belonged to a number of women's organisations, and was Publications Secretary of the Costume Society for twenty years, from 1974 to 1994.

Stan was the perfect gentleman, well-mannered, tall and handsome. He had the knack of making everyone he met feel at ease, men and women equally. Stan hardly ever got upset. In my eighteen years at home, I recall him losing his temper only once. Nellie, on the other hand, had an explosive temperament which frequently boiled over. She had deep feelings, but, in my experience, she had difficulty expressing them.

Despite their differences, or perhaps because of them, Nellie and Stan were a lifelong couple, faithful and devoted to one another. They celebrated their anniversary as Boxing Day, the day they first met in 1937. When they married in July 1940, Nellie, like both her own mother and Stan's mother before her, was expecting (me). Stan died in 1993, Nellie in 2001. It is a testament to their attitude to life that they produced four very different, highly individual and independent-minded children.

Stan produced hundreds of scripts, books and plays, but there was one writing job he failed to complete, despite promising to do so – *Nellie's Book*. This is the task I have set myself. My mother started writing the story of her early life in 1951, returning to it from time to time. She and Stan later paid a visit to Gibbon Street, Manchester, where she was born and brought up. Nellie's original title for her book was 'Empire Street'. She had a very clever explanation for this.

Nellie was a declared republican and had no time for royalty. To her, Buckingham Palace was 'that block of flats at the end of the Mall'. She was scathing about red velvet lavatory seats being provided for visiting royalty. When King George VI was crowned in May 1937, seventeen-year-old Nellie spent the day in bed to avoid the celebrations. In her teens, Nellie was a member of the Young Communist League and marched in favour of the Republican side in the Spanish Civil War. There is no way she would want to glorify the British Empire. And while 'Empire Street' – a terraced street in Manchester – sounds much like *Coronation Street*, for which Stan later became a script-writer, that is purely coincidental.

So why didn't Nellie simply call her story 'Gibbon Street', giving her home street its real name? In describing how the very poor 'managed' in the 1920s and '30s, Nellie was celebrating not just her own life, but the courage and steadfastness of hundreds of thousands if not millions of people for whom life was a daily struggle. Nellie recognized that her family and her neighbours were representative of a whole class of people who were at the very bottom rung of society. *Nellie's Book* is a hymn of praise for the men and women who brought up their families and lived a decent, law-abiding and often (although not in Nellie's case) God-fearing life, despite suffering grinding poverty.

In fact, Nellie chose the name 'Empire Street' with a deliberate double irony to it, social as well as political. It shows that Nellie could poke fun at her own class while praising their adaptability and fortitude. It was a standing joke with her that it was common in working-class homes to have two particular books on the shelf, both huge and worthy tomes, but just for show. Nobody actually read these massive volumes, and it was said that some even had bottles of whisky hidden inside. The two books? One was Leo Tolstoy's *War and Peace*. The other was Edward Gibbon's *Decline and Fall of the Roman Empire*. Hence 'Empire Street'.

After my mother Nellie died, following the death of my father Stan some years earlier, I inherited – with the agreement of my three sisters – a huge archive of diaries, letters, scripts and other writings of both our parents. Nothing was in any sort of order, and I had to piece together the script of Empire Street from various notebooks, pads and scraps of paper. There was a good deal of repetition. Not only did Nellie tend to write the same thing more than once, whenever she wrote a chapter of her book, that chapter would often include elements from several other chapters.

In piecing together Nellie's story, I have used her exact words and phrases as much as possible. I have done a good deal of re-arranging in order to make the whole a more logical and understandable narrative. Just occasionally, Nellie made spelling mistakes. These were rare, as befits a woman who astounded her teachers and her contemporaries by being able to spell 'chrysanthemum' correctly at the age of six.

Stan was well aware of his wife's literary efforts and realised that, while worthy of publication, they would first have to be heavily edited. In the daily journal he wrote for over forty years, Stan several times refers to 'Empire Street', promising to 'write it up'. He never did, despite being a highly productive writer. So here it is, based on her own words, Nellie's account of her early life growing up in industrial Manchester in the Depression years. It is truly *Nellie's Book*.

# 1

# *Earliest Memories*

Helen Colleen 'Nellie' Mape was born on 14 October 1919 at 76 Gibbon Street, Manchester, the family home where she lived for the first sixteen years of her life. Nellie was the fourth of eight children born to John (Jack) and Ada Mape. Jack, unable to work due to poor health, is variously described as a boiler fireman, mill foreman and general labourer. Ada, née Cottrell, was described as a cotton-mill weaver, for all that she worked as a spinner.

Jack and Ada were married on 5 April 1913 at St Brigid's Roman Catholic Church in the Bradford district of Manchester, not to be confused with the town of Bradford in Yorkshire. Jack was twenty-six years old, Ada just eighteen and heavily pregnant. Their first child, Annie, was born only seven and a half weeks later. A second daughter, Ada Mary, was born in 1915 but died the following year at one year old. Six months later, three-year-old Annie drowned in the canal near their home in Gibbon Street. Having lost her first two children at such an early age, Ada went on to raise six more. Nellie was the second-eldest surviving child, two years younger than Nora (Honora), who was born in 1917. After Nellie there was Winnie (b. 1922), John Thomas (b. 1925), Jean (b. 1929) and Bernard ('Mick') (b. 1931).

Jack's father, Patrick Mape, a self-employed labourer and journeyman galvanizer, was born in Ireland.[1] Patrick had settled in the Pendleton area of Salford with his brothers James and Richard, sisters Mary and Sarah, and their father Michael. Michael was a labourer and Mary a cotton operative. Mary had an illegitimate daughter, Eliza, who was born in 1885. The Mape family all came from Athny in what is now the Irish

Republic. They were possibly descended from Gerald Mape, heir of Henry Maperath of County Meath, a 'gentleman'. When Patrick Mape and Annie Lawler got married in 1877, the witnesses were Martin and Elizabeth Lawler. Apparently unable to write their names, the witnesses both 'made their mark' on the register.

The Mapes' tiny terraced house was demolished long ago, but Gibbon Street itself is still there. The street sign can still be seen on Alan Turing Way, almost directly opposite the new City of Manchester Stadium, home of Manchester City FC. Gibbon Street is now the access road to a giant Asda superstore, and also to another major sporting venue, the National Cycling Centre, otherwise known as the Manchester Velodrome. Stan, a keen racing cyclist in his youth, would have approved. In the 1920s and 1930s, the small terraced houses of Gibbon Street were dwarfed by the mills, factories and other industrial premises which took up the greater part of the street. The whole area was overlooked by the huge cooling towers of the massive Stuart Street power station just across the canal. The gates of the cotton mill where Ada worked were directly across the street from No. 76. The district was 'the grimiest, most densely populated and most built-up area of the city'.[2] Yet Nellie had great affection for Gibbon Street. It was her world and her university of life. She wrote:

> I arrived in Empire Street in 1919. I was of course a postwar baby, which may explain why I went through the whole of my school life as a member of that big class, over forty pupils as I remember. My intention, if not telling it the way it was, is at least telling it the way it looked to my young eyes. My book will not attempt any sort of statistical survey or would-be sociological analysis. It will simply be what one pair of (rather short-sighted) eyes observed and one pair of ears (very sharp) heard, and the small percentage still retained in an ageing memory.

I would love to have a fund of very early memories to call on. To be truthful, the first and almost the only thing I do remember from my toddler days is being wheeled in my trolley down a back street in Ancoats in Manchester by my father. He threw me the casual bit of information that 'people used to live in those cellars'. The only other fact I could recall about this exciting event was that I was wearing a bright-green, crocheted bonnet with very tight strings. This bonnet was subsequently dated by my mother as one she had made for me when I was eighteen months old, and I was probably two and a bit at the time and waiting for a place in the local nursery class.

My curiosity was aroused some years later when I was on a solo errand and recognized the street with the cellar dwellings. I clearly remembered the colour and rough texture of the bonnet, its tight woollen strings with bobbles under my chin, and my father's remark. I don't know where we were going that particular day. It was not on the route to Moston Cemetery, one of my father's favourite places of pilgrimage because this was the place where the Manchester Martyrs were buried. My father, a good walker despite his disability,[3] was much given to such expeditions. He liked visiting old churches and similar buildings, and may have been making for the Hidden Gem,[4] a beautiful little church in a back street off Albert Square. I remember going to Moston Cemetery during this period, walking some of the way, and being carried, then going part of the way by tram. Another place my father took me was to the Men's Club in Philips Park, opposite the Swan Pond. This was a small hut, perhaps for unemployed men, or for ex-soldiers, known as the Old Soldiers' Hut. Father played cards with his mates, while I spent my time clutching the railings round the swan pond and doting on the magnificent pair gobbling up the stale bread and occasional biscuits I gave them.

I had an older sister Nora, but she was of school age. At this time my mother was earning the family living in the doubling room[5] at the mill opposite our house. My father was unable to work as the result of an accident, but he looked after me well. My father liked cooking simple meals. In fact, the myth at the time was that all the men who had been in the war in France could peel potatoes and knock a bit of a meal together, but it probably was only a myth.

During the years that my father was minding me at home, I was naughty from time to time, but I would never say I was sorry. On these occasions I was banished to the back doorstep to think over my sins. I refused to repent a number of times, until I was eventually coaxed back in by some little treat. One of these bribes, I remember particularly, was a saucer of tiny new potatoes, a special treat. I was considered to have a large head and a round face, as my father's assorted nicknames for me indicated,[6] but the only contemporary photograph of me available shows that I was average size. The only other clear picture of my very early years comes not from my own memory of the incident itself, but from the oft-repeated tale trotted out at family gatherings by Aunt Dolly. She was a skilled raconteur, and the story went something like this: The setting was our living room, always known as 'the house'. Three earnest young women, my mother, the girl from next door and Aunt Dolly. Dolly was a grown-up cousin, but was always 'Auntie'. Dolly had been called in as arbiter of fashion, because she worked 'in town' and was therefore smart and up to date. Our dining table, stripped of its customary red chenille tablecloth, was spread with a length of mauve taffeta and covered again with flimsy tissue sections of a Weldon's paper pattern. Three anxious heads were bent over the table, trying to fathom it out. Quiet reigned outside, and concentration inside. As Dolly told it, she was nearest the open door, and remarked that she was sure she heard something go 'Flop!', followed by a dramatic pause.

In the telling of this tale at family gatherings, this word 'Flop!' was the signal for hysterical laughter. Quite why this was, I never understood. All that happened was the three of them went to the front door to find a crawling baby (me) scooting along the pavement towards the corner shop, instead of dozing safely on the sofa. That was all there was to it, but it was a hardy annual at seasonal family get-togethers for years afterwards. As I say, I was too young to remember it myself, but I like to think that I must have been keen to sample the delights of our own little world even before I could walk. This possibly helps to explain the fascination I had with my immediate surroundings, which never wore off in all the sixteen years I lived in Empire Street. That street and its two little satellite streets were my world, my playground and my education all in one.

I don't know what age I would have been before I considered myself capable of judging the merits or otherwise of the industrial street of Manchester in which I was born. Even in my toddler years I was able to appreciate the ample street-playing space of our long rows of two-up and two-down houses on one side, and the various mills and factories on the other. Traffic was mostly horses and carts, and so relatively safe. As I grew older, I realised that the greatest benefit was the absence of irate housewives opposite, shooing us off to 'play near your own house'.

At the age of six I was lucky enough to have a spell in Ancoats Hospital with a septic toe. I expect the nurses heaved sighs of relief when I left the hospital. The high sides of my hospital cot entirely failed to contain my six-year-old energies. When even the Irish girls grew tired of retrieving me from the veranda, I was judged to be ready for the convalescent home. I think I must have travelled to the convalescent home in a nightie, because when I got there I had to be fitted out with a complete set of clothing. Fixing me up with boots was a long job – I had small feet but fat legs, a difficult combination for the regulation knee-high black lace-ups. Eventually, kitted out to matron's satisfaction, I waited, awestruck, outside the doctor's door. I stood there, boots in hand, duly observing Matron's instructions: 'Go in, in your stockinged feet, stand up straight, and don't speak to the doctor.' I left my black shiny boots outside the door, conducted my side of the interview with nods and shakes, and emerged unscathed – to a bootless doormat! I pass over the ensuing uproar. I must have weathered it, and become shod somehow. After all, I learned the fox trot ('She's got some go in her, that one!') and to sing 'Under the Lilac'.

All went well until we had stewed tripe for dinner (which was every Thursday). I gave my next-door neighbour my weekly shilling to eat mine for me. She was so pleased with this financial success that she offered to 'find' my lost boots for me. After due negotiation, we closed the deal with a couple of liquorice bootlaces and a doll's mangle. The boots were beside my bed next morning, and fitted me better than before. As I went down to breakfast, I had to feel sorry for the bootless, stocking-footed child weeping outside Matron's office. I resolved to introduce her to my friend.

Nellie's father, Jack Mape, died on 30 March 1941, aged fifty-four. The causes of death are listed as cardiac failure, pulmonary tuberculosis and epithelioma of the skin of the back. His funeral on 5 April cost £13 10s, including 5s for the bearers. The undertaker's bill lists:

Polished coffin fully mounted, lined, bedded and pitched
Plate ornament and secured funeral rope
Motor hearse and two mourning saloons

Removal from Crumpsall Hospital
Inscription grave at Philips Park Cemetery

There is no doubt that Jack had a great affection for his daughter Nellie, at least as a child. Among my mother's things I found a postcard to her from Jack postmarked November 1925 when Nellie was six years old. It is from the Ancoats Convalescent Home, Great Warford, Cheshire. In simple print, Jack writes 'Dear Nellie, I hope you sing well at the concert. Daddy.'

When she was a little older, Nellie would visit her father in hospital. She thought she had to go to take him his newspaper from home, not realizing that this was simply a ruse by him to get her to visit him. Nellie would telephone her father from a kiosk when he was in hospital. She would go to the corner shop and borrow a vegetable or orange box to stand on, so that she could reach the telephone. Jack had many skin-graft operations, most of which were unsuccessful.

In his diary in June 1949, Stan records:

Wife's [Nellie's] father was a thoroughgoing rogue, but other people said he was very popular. When he was young he would gamble and drink his money away. He would bring women home, his drinking companions. There were awful rows. [Jack] had a terrible temper. He would throw his food on the fire. [Nellie] could manage him when she was fourteen. The girls were told to be in by ten, but stayed out until eleven.

Ma [Ada] left him three times, but she always came back. She was prostrate when he died. [He was] intensely jealous of his wife, who was fond of the gay life. [Ada] used to go round with a widow when Jack was in hospital. There were two other men, one called Reuben. Probably why he [Jack] used to come out of hospital before he was better.

10 FEBRUARY 1962:

Deficient communication and a time line thirty-two years later. Wife now realises that when she was ten and visiting her father in hospital at Crumpsall every Sunday, to take him the paper and his cigarettes and doing it for eight months, it was because <u>he</u> wanted to see <u>her</u>. She thought that for some peculiar reason he had to have the newspaper from home. (There were newspapers and cigarettes available in the hospital.) She also realises that the cook at the lodge, an Irish woman who agreed to take her in and send her a wonderful cooked meal ('saved from the doctors'), was probably very fond of her father and did it to please him. If it had been an unavoidable family chore for the girl, why did he not get Nora, the oldest girl, to do it? If only she [Nellie] had been told, 'Your father would love to see you', she would have been thrilled to bits.

13 OCTOBER 1964

Wife at the age of six, read that flowers and leaves breathe in the carbon dioxide that we exhale, went round carefully breathing on flowers and leaves.

8 NOVEMBER 1965

As a little girl, wife used to have great worries and not sleep at night (hence present anxieties.) Father talking about money & saying, 'That is the football club money', and she thought he had just helped himself and the police would put him in prison – not knowing he was the secretary & treasurer.

6 DECEMBER 1961

Wife's mother [Ada] died this morning. I woke about 7 a.m. and was aware of a strange and puzzling sense. Felt it had some significance. Wife's mother died at 8.30 a.m.

10 DECEMBER 1961

Funeral passed off very smoothly. Young Maureen [Nora's daughter] broke down completely afterwards. It was all too much for her – the coffin and the deep black hole. By her death Ada achieved what she had never done in life – all her children under one roof for a drink and a meal and family conference. (In fact she played them off one against the other and wanted to be the Queen of Spades with each family visited in turn.) It was the old story of the working mother. Wife remembers her dad doing all the meals (and the washing, but not very well). She wonders if she got interested in me because I cooked meals and served things up.

Ada died on 6 December 1961, aged sixty-seven. She had had eight children. Ada Mary and Annie died as young children, Winnie died in 1985, Nellie in 2001, Nora in 2002, John Thomas in 2004. At the time of writing, Jean and Bernard ('Mick') are still alive.

# 2

# *Home Life*

Nellie was able to recall with great clarity the details of her life at home: the furniture, carpets, curtains and bedding; washing, cooking and cleaning; and also how they ate their meals. Imagine living in a home with only one cold tap, just one gas light downstairs, and upstairs no heating at all and only candles for light. Whether or not you experienced this as a child yourself, imagine youngsters of today being made to go to bed at seven o'clock every night, winter and summer, up to the age of fourteen!

To beat her father's rigid curfew, Nellie would entertain her brothers and sisters with games and plays, all performed on the bed and often under the sheets. Given only an inch of candle to light her way to bed, Nellie would make her own candles from used candle-ends and string so that she could read in bed. At times the street outside would provide its own entertainment for the bed-bound Mape children. This is how Nellie remembered it.

Our own front room was basically like everyone else's. As well as the standard fireplace, there was a high, built-in cupboard with drawers underneath. There was a bright, pegged rug in front of the fireguard. There was no three-piece suite, but we did have a 'sofie' under the window. The living room had a fireside chair, a white-topped table, one or two wooden chairs and a stool or two. The one very basic fireside chair was for the master of the household. I never saw my mother sitting down. There were lace curtains and a blind at the window, and a large fitted cupboard to the right-hand side of the fireplace – a blackleaded range with polished steel edging. It was the done thing to have a sham blind at the top of the window, preferably with a crocheted border. A semi-opaque decorative paper covered the lower half for privacy. Our house had a pretty paper pattern showing swans and bulrushes.

All the kitchens in our row had a tall fitted cupboard, a twin of the one we had in our front room. In our house, this cupboard was completely emptied every Christmas, scrubbed out, and new shelf paper with frilly edging fitted from top to bottom. When it was dry, all the contents were put back exactly as before. This was a job I loved to do, though I was never keen on most other household tasks.

We boasted a rather ornate mahogany sideboard, 'bought new when we were first married', as we heard from our mother more than once. This piece of furniture was supplied with what seemed like dozens of little brackets, holding fancy little ornaments. I called these items 'little pot pigs' when discussing them critically with friends, and vowed I would never have any when I had a home of my own. [She didn't! – CFW] My father's wartime postcards from Flanders, some like the embroidered silk ones now so collectable, were in there. There were boxes of buttons and scraps of ribbons and lace. Best of all, on the top shelf there was a black bag containing a book about women's ailments. We understood we were not to refer openly to this book, which never saw the light of day in our presence.

Every house had a coal-hole under the stairs. There was a fireplace in both downstairs rooms, a gas cooker, and a brick-built fixed boiler in the kitchen which was heated by a coal fire underneath and shut in by a little iron door. This was our only source of hot water for washing clothes, and for our own washing and bathing. You filled the boiler with a bucket from the cold tap in the slop-stone alongside, and emptied it with a lading can, though some people used a sort of giant soup ladle with a wooden handle. It was very efficient, and not expensive to use. You could stuff anything that would burn into the fire under the huge copper boiler. In our street, a galvanized bath usually hung on a nail in the backyard. We probably had one, but I only remember an oversized enamel washing-up bowl, in which we were bathed until we were old enough to go to the municipal slipper baths every Saturday morning.[1]

The clothes rack, always full, hung from the ceiling. There was nothing much in the way of clothes storage, and I don't remember a wardrobe. Clean clothes were kept on the rack, and dirty washing was dealt with promptly. Clean clothes were simply taken off the rack and put straight onto us children. The front bedroom had a double bed and a single, plus, in later years, a large cot. Once a year, the flock beds were emptied and the ticking washed. To dismantle the bed, the metal criss-crossed laths had to be unscrewed before being disinfected.

Mostly, soap was bought as solid, brick-sized monsters. These had to be cut up for toilet purposes and shaved into shreds for the machines at the municipal wash-house, which was just coming into general use. The shavings then had to be blended with at least two powdered products, according to the beliefs of the mistress of the house. One of these was Monkey Brand panshine. There was also soft soap, ladled into a container.

Everybody had the same kitchen range in the living room, though it was never called that, just the fireplace. I can recall the smell of the Zebo blacklead which kept it bright. I remember the emery paper and the thick white polish which made the steel trimmings such a vivid contrast. We had a fireguard with a brass rail, but I envied the people who had a fender complete with fire iron, and, in the better-off houses, a fireside companion with a dear little shovel, tongs and hearthbrush hanging from hooks.

Mantelpieces usually had a plush fabric border with hanging bobbles if you could afford it, or otherwise whatever was the best you could do. There was no electricity in the Empire Street of my time – though it had begun to be talked about – but a man had been round canvassing for a special kind of gas fitment with automatic lighting. You pulled a chain on one side to light it, and another one on the other side to dowse it, as they used to say. We still had the bare gas mantle, so vulnerable to accidents with a carelessly applied match. The penny-in-the-slot meters applied to everyone, posh fitting or no. I don't remember anybody borrowing the traditional cup of sugar you so often read about, but people would ask their neighbours for pennies for the gas, especially on a Thursday.

Of the house interiors I knew well, only one family lived in the back while keeping the front room as a parlour. This was considered somewhat pretentious, as this family's lifestyle didn't exactly fit in with what was considered appropriate to having a parlour. One other house I visited fairly often to do errands for an elderly childless couple had parlour-style furnishing in the front room – carpet, plush curtains and a piano – but they did actually live in that room.

Not many people took a daily paper – the occasional granny allowed herself a *Daily Sketch*. Paper lads ran the streets with the evening papers. When father had a likely bet on, the children were instructed to listen out for the paper lad. There were no newsagents nearby.

Children were supposed to be seen and not heard. We were never ever allowed to butt in when adults were talking. Uninvited callers were never asked to sit down, but just stood near the door. Our mother did not care for gossip. She never 'neighboured', but neither did she ever refuse to give any help she could. It was scarcely a practical proposition for children to play inside the four-roomed houses. That was allowed only in special circumstances, like when you had a bad cold or were minding the baby. If you were minding the house, a well-behaved friend might be permitted for company. All houses were considered to need minding, for some mysterious reason. It was not fear of burglary – this didn't enter into it. During the brief maternal absences, when I was young enough to be 'playing house', I was allowed to have a friend in for company. We had a lovely time cutting up a carrot and any other suitable food item to make imaginary feasts.

As I approached fourteen, I was allowed to stay up on Saturday nights to mind the house when Mother and Father were out. My greatest joy was to take charge of the big iron pan of broth simmering on the open fire, and top it up when necessary. The amount I extracted, in my capacity as tester-in-chief, necessitated a great deal of topping-up before my parents returned.

Early to bed was the rule, and since the inch of candle allowed for undressing was soon used up, and no reading was therefore possible, the hidden details of domestic life in some of the very large families nearby provided endless material for silent speculation. Where did they all sleep? How did their mother get through all the washing? How did they all get round the table for meals? And so forth.

The night always began, according to my father's inflexible code, at 7 p.m., winter and summer. Children, he believed, should not be out at night. Therefore we went to bed at seven o'clock every night when he was at home, until we were fourteen years old. Few of the neighbours subscribed to this strict code, and we could hear the voices of lucky children playing 'I wrote a letter to my mother', and shrieking with mock fear as they whizzed round the gas lamp, clinging to the clothes line, for hours after we had nominally gone to rest.[2] We were in bed long before them, and we would have missed all the fun were it not for the fact that the sash window of our front bedroom gave us just the right angle of view. Early bedtime did not prevent us from pushing up the front window if anything exciting was going on in the street.

No gas was fitted upstairs, so we had no regular lighting in our bedrooms. Some people used oil lamps, but our mother thought these were dangerous and stuck to candles. When the children slept in the smaller back bedroom, they used a wall fitting like a vertical spike and triangular ribbed candles. Later, being moved into the larger front bedroom (as the family grew), ordinary, less interesting candles had to suffice, the strict allowance for undressing purposes each bedtime being a one-inch segment cut from a penny candle.

I liked to read at night, and it was a lucky day for me, a voracious reader, when a neighbour gave me a ball of real candlewick, suitable, she said, for string or for knitting. Some hope! As statue monitress at school, I had access to a treasure trove of burnt-out nightlights. This residue of wax converted easily into lumpy but usable candles for reading in bed. One advantage of the newly introduced waxed bread wrappers was that, tightly twisted, they made splendid torches for after-dark visits.

We did not, of course, even consider going to sleep. The big bed with a brass knob on each corner became at will, a tent, a palace, a ship, or even a zoo, to the great detriment of the sheets. When I played the roles of the animals, the orang-utan was considered my most natural characteris-ation. I shook the rails of the bedhead, and howled ferociously, until the littlest ones really were frightened.

From time to time, my mother would call up half-heartedly that my father would be 'coming up with the strap', but since we knew he did not have a strap, and was probably out anyway, we took little notice. If we were quite sure my father was out, we would send one of the little ones down with a request for a butty. Theoretically, we were not allowed any supper. However, an appeal for an after-hours butty was never refused in our house, though given with the inevitable proviso, 'You mustn't ask again'. We quickly learned the ploy of using the youngest child capable of delivering the request. It always worked, providing that Dad was not at home. Father had frequent long spells in hospital or convalescent home, and while he was away his iron rules were rather relaxed.

The others fell asleep more easily when the dark evenings came, but I have always had insomniac tendencies, and I so much liked to read. Special permission was occasionally given to stop out late at Belle Vue [Manchester's pleasure grounds] for the fireworks and pageant. The streets were never quiet, but howls and drunken singing were regarded more as entertainment than nuisances, and a good row soon collected an audience.

Old soldiers like my father were also all supposed to have terrible tempers, because of all they had been through in the trenches. Throwing their dinners at the back of the fire seemed to be a common symptom of this. I don't remember this particular thing happening in my own home – which isn't to say that it didn't – but I do have a picture of a bag of sugar blazing up after some overlong or over-extravagant Saturday afternoon shopping outing, and the consequent domestic recriminations.

It was considered an advantage to have a handy mother. Mine could knit and crochet, and she had a treadle sewing machine to run up dresses, etc. She could make vases out of old gramophone records, as many women did, and paper butterflies to pin on the curtains at Christmas. My mother was very good at this sort of thing, especially when it involved items of costume of her own handiwork, such as the 'celitroop tommy shanter' with a big satin bow at the side worn by a pretty workmate on a particularly successful 'chara' [charabanc] outing. This identified the year of that trip for ages afterwards when it came up in conversation.

The cotton mill opposite my house was never called anything but 'the mill'. My mother and one of my aunties worked there. Plenty of women seemed to be working in the 1920s, even if the men weren't.[3] They flocked out of the mill and other factories in Empire Street. I had a very hard-working mother. She did everything at great speed. Years later, seeing a cartoon character called the Tasmanian Devil, I was reminded of her as she 'sided up'. She would fold up the chenille tablecloth, cover the table with newspapers, and put the fire irons and any small movable items on top to clean them.

Holidays were unthinkable to most families in Empire Street. Much speculation went on about one somewhat reserved family who did have an annual week's holiday (always called 'going away'), when the father was said to be on two quid a week. They had a week at Blackpool every year, something very unusual for our street and a source of amazement to the neighbours. Presumably, the father worked overtime, or was earning a bonus, or possibly had a better-off relative.

Small families were looked on as a matter of luck. For example, 'They've only got the two' meant trips to the pictures or seaside if father was working. 'Only the one', on the other hand, was a matter for sympathy. Small families could also afford a camera, and thus had a valuable childhood record to gloat over, something we of larger, hard-up families had to do without.

Belle Vue Zoological Gardens was considered the cream of the 'day out' venues, and most people managed to get there at least once a year. At Belle Vue there was a big hall with tables and benches where you could eat your own food and buy drinks. Our packets of sandwiches were always the same, potted meat or salmon paste with a generous slice of factory cake on top. How I hated the veneer of bright yellow crumbs which clung to the top slice of bread! But I never suggested any alteration to the packaging.

It was a wonderful day out at Belle Vue, which was not too far from where we lived. Every animal was visited. You knew exactly where to find the bears and the bison. There was the museum with the skeleton of an elephant, and then there was the 'Ancient Ruin', to be climbed over and fantasised about. No thoughts of it as being just a crude sham of white-painted plaster entered our innocent youthful heads in those days. We even believed, at least temporarily, in the 'Rocky Mountain' scenery of the big rides.

Most children went to the pictures on a Saturday afternoon, while many mothers went to do their shopping 'on the market'. This was an arrangement which obviously suited both sides. Droves of children set off early, caring nothing for what might be showing that week. In any case, you could never be sure which cinema you would get into. It might be necessary to try several, and perhaps walk a considerable distance if queues were extra long. In our area, it was usually possible to get into the single superior (twopenny) picture house,[4] where the usherettes sprayed the aisles with disinfectant. But mostly our allowance was a penny for the pictures and a halfpenny to spend, so naturally we patronised one of the penny establishments, of which three were within walking distance.

Occasionally, if one had earned a little errand money in the week, it was possible to go to the twopenny cinema. Then we could enjoy the glorious moment when the serial began, and the giant word 'Collegians' would flash repeatedly onto the screen. The audience would roar out 'Kleejans! Kleejans!' and settle down to watch the antics of a batch of handsome American college boys. At the penny cinema we saw Charlie Chaplin, etc., but our favourites were 'Fat and Fin' (Laurel and Hardy) and community singing to the famous bouncing ball with 'I'm For Ever Blowing Bubbles' and so on.

Women did go on chara trips. I remember one to 'Eackly' (Heatley) near Warburton. Never having heard of the place, I enquired what was there to make it attractive, to be told 'a nice country pub' – result, one mystified child! Chara trips made for a little excitement in the street, even for those who were not going. Children were always allowed to stay up late to welcome their mums home and receive sticks of rock, toffee apples, dolls' dinners, etc.

Visits to the theatre were largely confined to the Christmas pantomime. I remember the pantomine at the Met [Metropolitan Theatre], with songs such as 'I Want A Pie With A Plum In', etc. There was the occasional bathing beauty contest, a charleston competition or talent show. The gallery of our only local theatre cost (I think) 4*d* for adults and 2*d* for children. Babes in arms went in free, so many very large babies accompanied their mothers. These 'babies' passed muster as long as they could be carried. The benches were packed as tight as they would go, no one daring to disobey the order to 'Shove up, there!' as late-comers arrived. In winter we occasionally got tickets for a musical entertainment at the Round House Theatre, such as Zuleika the Gypsy Maiden.

The local markets had their importance as a 'leisure haunt', with their naphtha flares[5] and humbug-making. Saturday afternoon was the time for 'getting your stuff' in for the week and was obviously a pleasure. The occasional rag rug for Christmas came from there. Full and varied as the locally available pleasures were, we did occasionally go further afield.

A little way along from the shoe shop was a butcher's with an open shopfront, where various assorted pieces of meat were auctioned on a Saturday night. 'I'll take any price,' was the butcher's cry, as he held up his arm, piece of paper on outstretched palm, nondescript mini-joint on top, presented to the less than enthusiastic pavement audience with the air of a connoisseur of the fine arts. There were various folk tales going the rounds of offers of a penny or even less for some succulent joint which the butcher was 'forced' to accept, supported by much juvenile interpretation of the law on this type of public transaction, along with dramatic accounts of the shopkeeper's anger and humiliation. Since the butcher was tougher and, as he was full of his own meat, presumably stronger than anyone in his audience, these stories seemed a trifle unlikely.

There was a chemist's shop on the corner, which although small was a palace of delights all the year round. I feel sure it must have had the customary glass flagons of jewel-coloured water, but I can't honestly say I remember them. I went there fairly frequently on errands and the smell was heavenly. Enormous trust was placed in the man behind the counter, and we honestly believed that he concocted the various remedies, 'believed in' by the residents of Empire Street, individually for each customer. The well-advertised patent medicines had very little standing compared with the Seven Oils, the Quassia Chips,[6] and the squares of camphor,[7] etc.

Our chemist liked to use his side window for an artistic display of one particular product or other, especially around Christmas time. Gill's Dentifrice and the Ivory Castles theme had a long and successful run with an exciting display of cardboard knights on horseback fighting the Giant Decay. The one I think I remember best was for Knight's Castile soap. This showed two beautiful Spanish lady figures, one blonde and one brunette. Both were magnificently costumed, one in white, one in purple. No wonder I was late for school almost every morning, magnetized by these gorgeous creatures.

The 'farthing shop' was the only one we knew of which would accept farthings for sweets, and only then in twos. We occasionally saw an illuminated tram, which was a great visual treat. If you put pins on the tramlines to be run over by the trams, they became miniature swords.

Big toys were only to be looked at in the Co-op Stores' windows. We aspired only to matchbox toys. One favourite purchase was a tiny doll, bath, towel and soap, all for a penny. We could get toffee tobacco, sweets that looked like cigarettes, chocolate 'smoking outfits' at Christmas, a 'lit' pipe, cigar, cigarettes and matches. All were sweets, but we could pretend we were actually smoking. A poor child's dream was a selection box of chocolate items.

In his diary of June 1949, Stan reports more of Nellie's memories:

House was infested with bugs and beetles. When you lit the gas the beetles would scuttle up the wall in thousands. They lived behind the wallpaper. Fond of wallpaper paste, flour, cracks, crevices, warmth, known as blackjacks. Kids hunted bugs with great glee. [Nellie] never minded them. [Her mother] spent a fortune on beetle powder 'cures' as they were called. Toscalon – wife thought for years it was a beetle powder, not face powder. Borax was the favourite killer.

# 3

# School Days

By her own admission, Nellie was always the youngest and bossiest in her class. She taught the 'Dunces', but argued with the teachers and consequently was denied the position of head girl. She was almost always top of the class, and she could and should have continued her education instead of leaving school at fourteen. Nellie took the scholarship (eleven-plus) a year early, but failed due to spending all her time on overlong answers to the first part of the exam. For some reason, she was not given the opportunity to resit a year later.

Nellie was intelligent, clever and determined, as is proven by the fact that she gained BA and MA degrees later in life. Her brother John, my late uncle, related that her form teacher would tell the class, 'If you all do half as well as Nellie Mape, you'll be doing very well indeed.' But Nellie clashed with her teachers and defied them. Missing out on the scholarship, low expectations for girls of her station in life, and the need to bring in a wage as soon as possible (Nellie being the second oldest surviving child in the family, and with a father unable to work) meant that she had to leave school to go to work as soon as she reached her fourteenth birthday. Fortunately, Nellie had a headmistress who inspired her and a form teacher who took her to the theatre. As a schoolgirl, Nellie took much of what she was told as the absolute, literal truth, causing some amusing misunderstandings. This is her account of her school days:

At the age of three, I was accepted into the nursery class in the infant department of the local non-Catholic school. My mother was still slogging away as a weaver in the doubling room of the nearby cotton mill, my father being unable to work. I loved it all, the slates and the chalks, the building blocks, the sand trays in which we wrote letters, the singing games and the simple dances. It seemed to me to be one long round of pleasure.

My favourite playthings were the glass jars of beautifully smooth cowrie shells. We used them for simple number work, and to make patterns. Our teacher told us that the natives in Africa (wherever that was) used these shells for money. As I played with the shells, I thought that such people must be extremely stupid. I knew what money looked like. Money was round and flat with the King's head on, like the halfpennies which occasionally passed through my hands. For years I puzzled to understand how the natives could use cowrie shells for money. I felt that somebody should point out to them how mistaken they were. I visual-ised the shopkeepers' disgust when offered shells in pay-ment, but I never had the courage to suggest to the teacher that somebody might enlighten these ignorant people. My ideas of commerce in Africa were somewhat naive.

Of course, I would not be rash enough to think that it was only when I went to school that my education began. However, I don't remember learning much before that, except that people used to live in the cellar dwellings in Ancoats. I heard this from my father as he pushed me by in my trolley.

We did have milk at school, eventually. Before that, I remember clearly the doting mothers passing hot mugs of cocoa through the schoolyard railings, along with biscuits and even an occasional slice of cake for this favoured small percentage of our schoolmates. I don't remember having any feelings of jealousy, but I might just as well have envied those children with good shoes or nice dresses. It was just part of the way the world was. I went hungry on most schooldays, but did not mention it at home.

At four years of age I was taken away (this was the teacher's expression – I gather she was very cross with my mother about it) from the nursery class near home and enrolled in the infant department of the local Catholic school. I was not aware at the time of any concession being made on the grounds of my being below the usual age of admission, but I gradually realized, as I moved up through the school, that I was somewhat younger than the others in my class. Eventually I became accustomed to the chant 'the youngest and the bossiest' in the class, a chant which followed me for most of my school life. No doubt I richly deserved it. Little remains with me of those early years, except one or two clear memories. When a thing puzzled me, it was often caused by my faulty interpretation of the words used. Usually I did not forget it for a long time, often finding the answer years later.

For example, in religious education in the first few weeks at school, when teacher read out 'and you *too* shall be saved', for ages I thought that she meant the two little girls in the front row, at whom she seemed to be looking. These two were pretty, well-dressed children, and I must have thought that it was not surprising that they had been chosen for the honour. Another time, reading from a story, the teacher referred to 'a plump little girl'. When none of us could explain what 'plump' meant, she illustrated the word by lifting me up onto the desk, saying 'This is a plump little girl.' Whether the other children got the point I do not know, but certainly I did not.

In my first couple of days at this school, we were all given a piece of paper (presumably a blank form) to take home for our parents to write down our names and addresses. I was very contemptuous of this. I knew my own name and address, although I am not sure if I would have been able to write it at that stage. I wondered why the teacher did not simply ask each child for the information, but the ways of teachers were a mystery to me then, and remained so for most of my school life. I remember the alphabet cards on the wall: A is for apple, etc. D was a drummer boy. I always thought he was facing the 'wrong' way, i.e. he was walking from right to left. I could read a little before I went to this school, a skill I picked up in the nursery class, but I was very downcast when I was unable to fathom out the word 'ONE' on the blackboard. It looked like 'OWN', but I knew it wasn't that. None of the others could say it either, but that was little consolation. I suspected this was one of my new teacher's annual triumphs over the reception class.

When we were a little older, and hopefully a little more mature, we were allowed to join the pupils of the big school over the way for their annual concert. This was always a big success. Our musical number was 'Follow Suzanne', a tribute to the famous French tennis star Suzanne Longleu [Lenglen]. We wore white dresses and pumps, sported tricolour headbands and carried Woolworth's tennis racquets. As we danced, we sang:

> Follow Suzanne, follow Suzanne
> All the boys are falling to a man.

I was visualizing the scene literally as usual and as usual getting it all wrong. The 'boys' I saw as little lads in shorts, tilting and falling forward towards a tall man, like some skilful gymnastic exercise by a row of Kelly dolls. I did not mention this to anyone. I hated to be laughed at, which I frequently was if any adults were around when I uttered this kind of naive remark.

After this thrilling taste of theatricals, we were all only too eager to move over to the big school at the appropriate time. This two-storey building dated from about 1870 [actually 1893]. There were four classes in the downstairs hall, with the headmistress's office and two classrooms leading off it. Upstairs was one large hall, divided into three by sliding partitions, and a stage at one end which also doubled as a class from time to time. We sat on backless forms, attached to long desks. There was no staffroom, as far as I ever knew.

I remember an early history lesson while still in the big hall, so I must have been about seven at this time. We were learning about the Roman invasion of Britain. How I hated those Romans! With my unfortunate propensity for visualizing scenes and taking words literally, I pictured the Romans wading ashore from their boats, protected by their armour. Each Roman would raise a powerful leg and push one of the Ancient Britons, who were of course all old and helpless, flat on his back into the water. This was my naively literal interpretation of the way the natives were 'de-feeted', each conquered by an enormous Roman foot in a strong leather sandal.

In the same class I volunteered the opinion that 'Caledonia, stern and wild' was in America. I had confused it with California. The teacher did not laugh – all credit to her. In the next class, further round the hall, I felt very resentful when my answer that Manchester was on the River Medlock was rejected in favour of the River Irwell. I knew that the Medlock flowed through Manchester, as I had seen it. I hated the idea of our river being demoted to a mere tributary.

I was slowly developing an undesirable habit of wanting to argue with the teacher. This tendency led to a tremendous clash later on with the arithmetic and sports teacher, a flame-haired lady with a temper to match. This was an encounter which broke me of the habit, and gave way to much more appreciation on my side. I yearned to be a monitress and give out pencils and drawing materials, but I had lost my stripes in class one. Then, when I was put in charge of watering the beans resting on the top of the solid-fuel stove in the hall, I drowned them, rotting the flimsy container and spilling the soil all over the floor.

I still hoped, however, and a year later I was allowed to take the cubes and pyramids out of the cupboard when we were having a shading lesson. This was after teacher had approached me to borrow what she described as a 'lovely little cap' she had noticed me wearing, and wished the class to draw. Ugh! The lovely little cap in question was a perfectly plain, crocheted coral-pink one. It was, in my eyes and everyone else's apart from teacher herself, entirely without interest. She pinned the cap to the blackboard, pointing out its interesting texture, light and shade, etc. I knew she was wasting her time. Everyone hated having to draw it, all the more because it belonged to me. I was never a popular girl, except in one or two small areas, and I can quite understand why.

To my great satisfaction, I eventually became paint monitress. I collected up the three-section paint saucers and washed them in the little corner sink on the landing in ice-cold water. So we progressed through the classes, learning to knit (some of us), to embroider, to learn poetry by heart, to dance 'Gathering Peascods',[1] to wrestle with fractions, and to put heart and soul into rehearsals for the annual concert. Our sights were set on the top classes, which were called forms one, two, three and four. The top classes seemed to us to elevate our elementary school way above the other such schools in our neighbourhood, and put us almost into the Angela Brazil bracket.[2]

Our headmistress Miss O[3] was tremendously go-ahead, and did wonders for the school. I admired her enormously, though she never took to me. We knew that the four top classes, especially form four, were first in the queue for any little treats that were going, and in particular the week's camping in Heaton Park, which always went to the top class.

As our headmistress explained to us, everyone got to the top class eventually, and so everyone got their turn. When we moved into this privileged section, we learned home management, had a netball team, and had swimming and singing lessons every week. We learned to cut out materials and to use the single sewing machine. Eventually, nearing the top of the school, we went to another school for cookery, and later for laundry. Lucky us! 'One iota' was an expression often used by our sports mistress Miss Lee, as was 'knock them into a cocked hat', referring to netball matches which we seldom won.

In this top half of the school, we had teachers who specialized in their subjects, unlike the little ones, who had the same teacher for everything. The flame-haired lady was in charge of form three, and took us all for sums, swimming and netball. Next door a gentle, youngish teacher taught history, art and music. This last subject, music, was the only one I actually disliked. My heart sank when our music teacher unrolled the calico sheets of tonic sol-fa exercises [the musical scale: doh, ray, mee, fah, soh, lah, tee, doh] and embarked on a dreary half-hour of attempting to get us to sing the groups of notes as she indicated them with her long pointer. This lesson was quite separate from singing, which I thoroughly enjoyed, with the headmistress at the piano on the stage playing such airs as 'Linden Lea, Arise, O Sah.' Fortunately, my less than attractive singing voice was lost among the others. This was not like another time, away from school, when I joined a youth choir and was requested to mime the words in future.

The third of these partitioned classrooms was presided over by a good-tempered young woman whose specialities included dressmaking (starting with an apron, of course), health, diet, and home management. We had regular lessons from an elderly district nurse, who showed us how to bath a baby. We practised on a large celluloid doll, and, when some generous-hearted mother could be persuaded to lend one, with a real live baby. There was an exam at the end of the year on the care and feeding of infants, with a copy of *The Wind in the Willows* for the child with top marks. When my year took this exam, they decided to give a paperback textbook instead. I lost the book, but saved the reward label, which amused my own children when it came to light. My mother was far from amused at the time, when I tried to thrust my newly acquired ideas on budgeting and healthy living on her.

Arriving in the top classes was not all joy. We found this out in forms three and four when the annual trip to the seaside came round. The headmistress decided that every senior girl had to take charge of a younger one for the whole day. We were not allowed to choose, but had one allocated to us, like it or not. However, the annoyance that this caused was somewhat alleviated, as we were about to set off for New Brighton. The parents of our charges, coming to see them off, pressed bags of sweets and sixpences and shillings on us, saying how much they appreciated what we were doing.

Nevertheless, we muttered to each other that no one had taken care of us when we were in the lower classes. I remembered, though I wished I hadn't, the inevitable essay, following a previous year's trip to Southport in which I described being told to 'go behind the sand dunes' for an essential purpose. I was sent round to each teacher in turn on that occasion, to show them my essay, with no idea why.

I liked school and did not look forward to the time when I must leave. Strangely enough, I did not seem to mind when I did not get a grammar-school place, in what was called the scholarship, although I had been expected to get one. I was ten, and it was suggested that I could try again the next year, but this never came up. When I began my own teaching career some forty years later, I realized why I had failed. I had answered the short questions on the first half of the English paper at great length – I only woke from my trance when the supervising teacher came to tell me that the time was up – but I had not written one word of the essay.

I was not conscious of being overly conceited, but I am sure that I was. I expected to be top of the class in any subject requiring written answers and a good memory. I was barely average in arithmetic, hopeless in art, and I never learned to knit correctly. I was almost always late for school, despite the efforts at home to get me off in good time. I was a dreamer, and, except when crossing the main road, I usually tried to read a book as I went along. This did not matter so very much until Lent, when we assembled every morning for special prayers in the hall. Every minute late meant you had to go to the head-mistress's study afterwards for the strap, which consisted of a gong and a wooden coat-hanger.

One stroke on the palm was the penalty for latecomers, with more for talking in class, giving cheek and so forth. I was only in real trouble twice in my school years, and did not get the strap on either occasion. First, I was reported by some anonymous person for attending a 'non-Catholic club', a temperance society [the Rechabites: see Chapter 7], and was called before the headmistress. A girl from another class was called into the headmistress's study at the same time for a similar purpose. She belonged to something called, I think, 'The Woodcraft Folk'. I don't know how she got on, but I did not give up my membership of the Rechabites. Nevertheless, I worried all the time that I would be found out and reported again.

I was always scared to death of the head after this. I heard her say to the unknown man who was present at the interview (about my membership of the Rechabites) that she had never trusted me because I never looked her in the eye. This was quite true. Some years before, she had dramatically described, in her weekly talks to the whole school, how an abusive mother had rapped her knuckles on Miss O's 'nick', indicating the bright red skin above the modesty vest which filled in the space above the 'v' neckline of her dress. This space drew me like a magnet, and I always focused my eyes on it if I had to address her.

The other time I was in deep trouble was after an argument in the schoolyard lavatories. Lily Ford had occupied a cubicle for longer than was reasonable, as others were waiting. She eventually emerged to see me writing on the wall and reported me for writing rude words. What I actually wrote was 'LFPL' ('Lily Ford's Private Lav'), supposedly to indicate that Lily had appropriated the cubicle for private use. When the head teacher came bursting into the class shortly afterwards, she made a three-act drama out of it. She told us that she had been to inspect the scene of the crime, and could not believe what she was reading, and had never been so disgusted in her life.

I could not believe that she would actually go into that somewhat bleak and unsavoury place, where to my knowledge the worst that she would see was 'X loves Y'. I tried to defend myself (I don't think I knew any rude words), but I was sobbing too bitterly to get the words out. I was ordered to stand at the front of the class for the rest of the lesson. My own teacher was very sympathetic, letting me stand behind the blackboard. Even Miss Redhead came through from next door to add her condolences. I did not get the strap, but a letter in strong terms was sent to my parents. Another letter was sent to the parents of my best friend Eileen, who was not involved in the incident. I was forbidden to walk home with her from school for the rest of the term.

It would be nice to be able to say that Miss O might just have changed her opinion of me, when (because of the age gap) I had to do an extra year in the top class. Having 'done all the work before', as the teachers frequently said, it was handy to be able to send me on errands, to take an occasional class of little ones, to post letters, buy flowers for the altar and so forth. All this might have put me in a better light, but no! When I was sent by my form mistress to the head with a message to say that I had been chosen to be headmistress's monitress for the year (the nearest we got to a head girl), I was given a return message: 'Ask your teacher to choose another candidate.'

The form mistress for the top form was very good to me, although a lot of the girls were terrified of her. She was an elderly lady with a curly 'front' such as Queen Mary wore. The tale about this hairpiece, as I presume it was, was that she had rescued a girl from a blazing gas cooker and consequently had to wear a wig. She encouraged us to read. Once a week in class, she would ask us what book we were currently reading. When I said *Jane Eyre*, she said it was unsuitable, and I must not read any more of it. When the next occasion came round, I said *Jane Eyre* again. She was very angry and said it was an immoral book.

Whenever she rebuked me in class, my eyes filled with tears, as much as I hated this to happen. This time she turned away, muttering scornfully about me 'turning on the waterworks'. However, it was very seldom that I was in her bad books. She kept places in class religiously, as in a Victorian school story, but based on a running total of marks for a month's written work rather than answers in class.

We had thick exercise books backed by her in brown paper, with a great black number on the cover. She returned them to us in class in numerical order. I had been number one for so long that I was somewhat taken aback after a spell at home with bronchitis to find a giant curly figure nine on my book. Actually, this did me some good with my schoolfellows in showing how fair 'Scallywag' (her nickname) was. It didn't take too long for me to get to the top again. My teacher must have listened carefully when I read.

Friday afternoons were very popular with everyone. Teacher always read us a serial. We had *The Old Dominion*, *The Scarlet Pimpernel*, and *The Woman in White*. Occasionally, she would ask me to carry on with the reading while she attended to something else. She would tell the class that they must be quiet, and that I would write on the board the names of any persons who spoke. They did not doubt that I would do just that, because I had been known to do it before. In fact, I think they kept quiet so they could hear the story, irrespective of who was reading it. They could always make cutting remarks after school. I was amazed when reading *The Scarlet Pimpernel* years later to work out that the evil French spy was not called 'Shovel On'!

Another of teacher's kindnesses was taking us to the theatre several times in the shilling seats, for which she would collect small instalments. We saw Martin Harvey in *The Only Way*, *Where The Rainbow Ends* and *King Lear* – quite an assortment. I cried so desperately during King Lear that a lady on the row behind comforted me with a box of chocolate almonds – I shared them, of course. Having seen what a real play was like, I declined to show my teacher the scripts of my backyard plays, which she had somehow come to know about. I had just enough sense to know that they were no good, and I could imagine how disappointed she would be.

She taught us copperplate handwriting, and supplied us with special nibs out of her own pocket. She entered us for the *News Chronicle* handwriting competition. To my astonishment, she took out a little penknife and scratched out one stroke of my entry which was not up to standard. She turned round the knife and smoothed the paper with the pearl handle, and invited me to redraw the offending items. I did win a prize, though not the top prize. No policeman called at the school, thank goodness, to denounce me for my 'crime'.

Several times in my last year at school I supervised a class of little ones when their teacher was absent. More frequently, in English lessons I responded to the appeal to 'see if you can do anything with the "Dunces"', openly referred to by this nowadays unthinkable title. This group of six or eight girls, whom I knew very well, were known to teachers and scholars alike as the 'Dunces'. They were my especial charge in English lessons, and they actually welcomed my help with compositions. Far from resenting me, as many of my other classmates did, they formed the nucleus of my playtime companions. They took part with obvious enjoyment in what I can only describe as a five-day soap opera. This was a dramatised version of every story-book I had ever read, of which there were many. Even when I was an established big girl, playtimes were always a pleasure. The 'Dunces' were also regular members of my playground dramas, part role-play, part unscripted, but unwritten.

For the indefatigable Miss O, the annual school concert could prove the most nerve-racking and expensive event. At school, everything had to give way to the concert. As well as the costumes to pay for, there would be at least shoes or pumps to provide. Pumps were compulsory, but one or two home-made substitutes cobbled together from old felt hats passed muster without comment.

Our poor teachers! Everyone's timetable was in tatters. The casting alone must have been a nightmare to those with a social conscience. I hope they never encountered a child from a very poor home with enormous talent, as in the girls' comic papers. If such a child were to be subsidized, all the others would know that they couldn't have afforded it. Pointed talk, if nothing worse, would be sure to follow. In practice, choosing the principal performers was no problem. These favoured few usually learned toe-dancing, and were thus equipped to fulfil the audience's expectations of thrilling highlights and an artistic finale. And, with fathers in decent jobs, the family could well afford a costume for each number, and could even pay for the occasional hired outfit.

This is not as snob-ridden as it sounds, and no resentment was shown towards these multi-costumed favourites of fortune. It was all part of the natural order of things. Some of us could shine in other areas of school life and you didn't hear the nobs grumbling about that. So the rehearsals continued. One girl offered to lend her 'low quarters' for a character part, which completely baffled the teachers, and set us even more firmly in the belief that teachers did not seem to live in the real world.

Then came the dress rehearsal. There was an all-out strike by the top class, who refused to go on, and were all crying buckets behind the stage. The trouble was that the costumes for their Irish number, adhering faithfully to their teacher's design, looked like nothing more than plain white cotton pillowcases equipped only with the necessary neck and armholes, each dress adorned with a giant green satin shamrock across the front. Some compromise was evidently arrived at. Maybe the unflattering hemline was shortened, or green sashes were added to make a bit of shape. Whatever it was, they did go on each night, and were very well received, we were told. In contrast, the 'Sleepy Time Down South' beach pyjamas of we younger ones went down very well with us. At the end of our number, three rows of very satisfied little girls composed themselves to rest on the slowly darkening stage. At this point, the audience erupted with inexplicable mirth, and a voice from the wings muttered 'I'll kill that child.' Apparently, yours truly, blissfully luxuriating in her fashionable flared trousers, centre front, had been acting her socks off as a sleeping 'Southern infant', and had to be demoted to the back row for subsequent performances.

Once a year the girls in the top forms had a whip-round for their teacher's Christmas present. A delegation trio was appointed to make preliminary enquiries at the chemist's about the price, availability and appearance of this most important purchase. We never considered anything other than a scent spray, the biggest and most ornate we could get for the available funds. The negotiations were drawn out for as long as possible. To be permitted to handle perhaps half a dozen possibles, and to receive a puff from the demonstration spray, was pure delight.

Our local chemist never failed to offer a scent card for each of the contributors, and never insulted us by suggesting something different. It never entered our heads that since a scent spray was the traditional present for teachers, each one must have an accumulation from previous years. During preliminary discussions, alternative gifts were occasionally suggested, usually by girls who had no intention of contributing, but once toilet soap had been ruled out (on the grounds, incredible as it seemed to us, that teachers used scented soap every time they washed), it was back to the scent spray with sighs of relief all round.

I was in the top class for two full years and an extra half-term (November 1933) until after my fourteenth birthday. This was because, for reasons unknown, I went through the school younger than my classmates. Aged 12/13 years, first year in top class 1931/2; aged 13/14 years, second year in top class 1932/3; left school, November 1933, aged fourteen. Because my fourteenth birthday fell in mid-

October I was not able to leave school until the November half-term. We broke up on a Wednesday. A few days beforehand, I was informed that a man, unknown to me, had visited the headmistress and had given me the only office job then available in the area, in the local steelworks.

Having an office job to go to, to the envy of my classmates, I started work the next morning. It was a Thursday. The job was in the progress office of this large steelworks where only men and boys had worked before.[4] There was no preliminary interview. I started work on the Thursday at 7.45 a.m., my clocking-on card ready in the rack, my wage fixed at nine shillings a week, with a shilling rise after twelve months. I had to go to evening classes, for which, if your attendance record was complete, the firm would repay your fees. Alas, I was never in this happy situation. I loved English night but hated arithmetic and missed some of the classes. Thus ended my days of schooling. My adventures in the world of work had begun.

## Back to School

The *Bolton Evening News* of 29 August 1968 headlined the news that Mrs Helen Wood, 48-year-old mother of four, had just won a place at Manchester University to take a degree in history, English and Drama. 'This personal triumph comes as the climax to four years' hard study at Bolton Technical College. Mrs Wood had elementary education in Manchester and used to work in the Civil Service and market research "in between bringing up my four children". She says, "All that time a desire for education was burning in me, and I knew I would have to do something about it soon. It would have seemed ridiculous four years ago to be doing this, but I'm quite confident now."'

In 1965 Nellie gained five 'O' levels, including English Language and English Literature. This was at the age of 45. She took her 'A' levels over the next two years, gaining passes in English, history and geography, but was denied admission to university in 1967 and so continued with A' levels 'to keep my hand in'. She went to Manchester University as a mature student in 1968, gaining a BA in Drama and English in 1971 and an MA in 1978.

# 4

# *Playing the Lead*

Nellie read to her class in school, performed in the school concert and made up stories for the other children, enthralling them with her continuing 'soap operas'. She also entertained her brothers and sisters with bedroom games and stories, and roped in other children for her theatricals in the backyard, back street or any handy open space. She was the writer, producer and chief performer. Nellie was, in embryo, an actor-manager. She had an early interest in and love of costume that lasted all her life. She was in charge of wardrobe for the Manchester College of Education production of Tennessee Williams's *Suddenly Last Summer*. At Manchester University, she helped with the costumes for several plays and in 1972 had a small part in Brecht's *Baal*.

In addition to putting on her own 'productions', even taking the lead in the first act of *King Lear*, the young Nellie organised the annual May Queen procession. She ran her own informal knitting club and 'rainbow club' on the steps of the local shop. Most of all, Nellie was 'boss of the street' – the girl who took the lead in street play and expeditions to the park. Nellie took on the job of marking out the soccer pitch where her dad's team played. She also wrote out the team lists. Here's how she described her various roles:

As well as the school concert, which finished the social round for the year, there was also a minor affair for the pupils only, just before we broke up for Christmas. In my last year at school, the top class (thirteen-year-olds) gave the first act of *King Lear*. This was not a wise choice, considering the rows of seven- and eight-year-olds on the front benches.

I was Lear, and made my own costume from an old red dressing gown and a generous hank of crêpe hair. To my astonishment, the 'old chap' was greeted with cheers and applause. My painfully memorized speeches could scarcely be heard. Our own teacher was furious, even when enlightened later, utterly failing to appreciate that the atmosphere of the festive season and the familiar red outfit and long white beard had conveyed a highly original interpretation of Shakespearian tragedy to our inexperienced audience. Who now could doubt the enormous influence of appropriate costume in aiding dramatic appreciation?

As I have mentioned, far from resenting me, as many of my other classmates did, the 'Dunces' I occasionally taught formed the nucleus of my playtime companions. Every playtime began with eager cries of 'Where are we up to?' This seemed to go on for months. I was not a creative or imaginative child in any way, and all my plots were derived from storybooks. There were lots of pirates, hidden treasure, fair maidens to be rescued from wicked knights and so forth. Damsels in distress were let down imaginary ropes as they clung to the window frame of the men's club in one corner of the schoolyard.

Few specific plots remain in my memory. They largely consisted of kidnappings, the storming of medieval castles, and innocent heiresses being forced to marry black-hearted villains. I never matched the ingenuity of my own children in later years. They would while away long holiday trips in the back seat of the car with similar long-running sagas, minus the playground dashing about, but adding original songs to which I never aspired.

During my last couple of years (twelve to fourteen) as a street child, I would take groups of younger children to the park. I usually supervised our street games, and I held clubs on the corner-shop step. In the two or three years during which the organisation of the Empire Street May Queen fell to my lot, I debated my choice of leading players, designed and made the tissue-paper costumes, turning the cuttings into aptly named artificial flowers for the garland, and rehearsed the rigmarole of sung snippets customarily used down our way. For all that, I foresaw no benefits further ahead than the party in our backyard (with white *and* brown bread) provisioned from the tin full of pennies we usually collected.

Still decidedly lacking in original ideas, I used well-known historical episodes, such as Queen Elizabeth and Walter Raleigh's cloak, Alfred and the cakes, etc. On one backyard occasion, a smaller child ruined the performance of the Elizabeth and Raleigh cloak episode with 'oh, this dastangly puggle', being unable to pronounce it any other way. I was unable to wean the youthful actress playing the Tudor Queen from 'Oh, this dastangly puggle', and had to put up with it.

I adapted stories from cheap children's publications. Here the problem was the delivery 'with expression' taught at the local school (not my own), or at temperance society meetings. Unfortunately, the local school believed in putting a lot of expression into reading aloud, and this spilled over into my neighbour Ivy's rendering of my adaptation of a Cornish smuggling tale (I had no creative imagination). It resulted in 'I *must* go to Penzance, *with* this cream *for* the market, before 8 o'clock', at what was supposed to be a dramatic crisis. This was made worse by her misreading of my handwritten script as 'Penzanee', and I was too cowardly to correct her. Ivy was always a stalwart member of my rainbow club on the corner-shop doorstep, and she took a leading part in my backyard play readings. My teacher somehow learned about these backyard plays and asked me to show them to her. I had just sufficient judgement to know they were no good and declined her kind offer.

In addition to these scripted backyard performances, we also indulged in improvised two-handers in one of the large boilers on the croft. These were empty ship's boilers, waiting on the croft for their turn to be repaired. We always played rich society ladies. All I can recall of this activity are the elaborate preparations, all in mime, of my fellow participant. She would do her hair, apply make-up and perfume, give orders to the chauffeur, etc., before announcing that she was off to the 'Ee-lightee' (Elite) Dance Hall. I wasn't all that well up in society small talk myself, but I always cringed at that, although I was too cowardly to say anything.

Much of the time allocated to any of our two-handed 'productions' (there was no audience, of course) went on elaborate preparations. We arrayed ourselves in imaginary luxury garments, did up our exaggeratedly long hair, and dabbed on invisible face powder. We knew enough to mime use of a scent spray from the usual Christmas offerings to class teachers, and we sprayed 'scent' lavishly on any supposedly receptive surfaces. Another of my friends, Edna, had learned from *Peg's Paper*,[1] or some similar literary source, that the latest thing was to dab behind the ears for glamour. We religiously observed this ritual.

The ceremony was punctuated by frequent enquiries and trips to the 'window' to see if the big posh cars of our imagination had arrived. We never seemed to go to the same function. My destination was usually Lady Somebody's reception, Edna preferring the 'Ee-Lightee'. When Ivy joined in my favourite pretend games, she enthusiastically dolled herself up, powdering her nose, spraying herself with perfume, all in mime, as she made ready for the big car which was to take her to the 'Ee-Lightee' Dance Hall. The men's club, a prefabricated building which backed onto our playground, was very useful. We fitted

imaginary ropes to window frames to rescue screaming maidens and escape from the 'villains'. At home, we children had the back bedroom with its brass-knobbed double bed. This was the setting for endless bedtime dramatic play with characters such as Cleg Kelly, hero of S.R. Crockett's *Knight Errant of the Sheets*.

The May Queen required access to a long dress and a lace curtain for her train, and, most desirable of all, lots of doting aunts and uncles within easy distance. This last item was not easy to achieve, but boosted the takings in the collecting tin in a good year. We had a little ad-hoc committee for these early decisions, but after that all the arrangements were in my hands – at least they were when I was running it.

I was able to organise and conduct a knitting club, using the broad doorstep of the corner shop as headquarters, and to go to the play centre at a school about a mile away. Nowadays parental excuses still crop up from time to time, excusing noisy groups of children on council estates and so forth, pleading that there is 'nothing for them to do'. We never heard this expression in my young days. You only had to walk out of your own front door and say 'What are we playing?' to the unelected but undisputed person in charge, usually a girl about eleven or twelve years old – the 'boss of the street'. This much-respected position became vacant as she attained fourteen years and went to work. This was one of the unwritten rites of passage to the lower regions of adulthood, along with the need to go on errands.

No official title was awarded to the young lady in this supervisory position. If younger, pushy children – perhaps newcomers – attempted to dispute her authority, they were quickly told, 'You're not the boss of the street.' The boss's position was thus defined without argument. I don't remember any discussion beforehand as to one's suitability. The 'leader' just seemed to emerge from the pack, like the

Conservative leader up to a few years ago. If the boss girl did not happen to be present, the children might start a game anyway, but this often led to arguments, so the other way was better. Occasionally we invented our own singing games, but these did not have the lasting power of the traditional ones, which soon returned.

One of my great pleasures was connected with the games of football on the croft. As soon as I was old enough to be trusted, I was allowed to mark out the pitch using a little whitewashing machine on three wheels. You made up the mixture, poured it in, turned on the tap, and trundled it along last week's faint outline. The white fluid ran over the front wheel, and the job was done.

More than sixty years later, I saw an almost identical machine [line marker] on television. I had this privilege because my father was an official of the local church football team, which had a high reputation in the area. They were known for winning cups and trophies.[2] I also printed out the names of the teams on the team sheet, always remembering to add A.N. Other. My literal interpretation of what I was told as a child often caused me some anxiety. In a drawer at home, there was some money set aside, which was said to be 'the football club's money'. With hindsight, I can see this was normal practice with officials of voluntary organisations. I somehow got it into my head that my father had taken this money. For years I worried that the police would come round for him, but they never did.

## Street Games

For Nellie's generation, children's play and recreation were completely different from today. For a start, there was no television and, for most, no radio either. In all her writings, Nellie

never mentions her family having a radio. In later life, Nellie delighted in owning her own radio in its handsome mahogany case, which we children were strictly forbidden to touch. It was quite clear it was her radio and for her exclusive use. The only concession I got was to be allowed to listen to *Children's Hour* every afternoon after school. My strict instructions were that I had to switch on the radio only as the programme was about to start, and switch it off immediately at the end.

Poor children of Nellie's generation had few toys and generally made their own amusements. As houses were small and crowded, children mostly had to play outside. Nellie thought it a great privilege to have the pavement opposite her house, which flanked the cotton mill where her mother worked, as a playground. There were the pavements, the backyards and back lanes, the canal, open spaces and playgrounds, all close at hand. Nellie and her contemporaries used anything they could find for their games. As the recognised 'boss of the street', Nellie dictated which games would be played and where her gang of children would go. But she also enjoyed playing on her own.

We children found plenty to occupy ourselves in street games: hop-flag [hopscotch], skipping, simple acrobatics, and playing house for the younger ones. This last popular pleasure largely depended on the fortuitous acquisition of a stick of chalk with which to draw furniture on the pavement. These artistic efforts adhered strictly to tradition, just like the drawings of houses by all the children I ever knew: central door, four windows with looped-back curtains – nothing like the four-room terraced dwellings in which we all lived. Children made all their own activities, unless things happened in the street, whereupon we would push up to the window and enjoy the show.

One vivid thing remains in my mind. There was a large flagstone on the opposite side of the street. It was part of the pavement and was very large and smooth. There were no houses on that side of the street, only the mill. I thought I was very fortunate in playing there. I would lie on my stomach and draw on that flagstone, although I was not very good at it. My favourite thing to draw was the school outfit: gymslip and two blouses, and an attaché case with my initials on. This represented the acme of desire. A lump of clay made a shop, boiled ham and rolls of bacon, and cakes with a slice cut out to show they were cakes. You would roll the 'boiled ham' in brick dust to make it look like real ham. Then you would stick a matchstalk in, and that was the bone. The currency for playing shop was broken bits of crockery, priced according to pattern.

I could play all day on that one little bit of flagstone. I had a piece of slate to draw with, but no bright chalks, just the occasional charcoal or bluestone. I would draw my house in outline on the pavement, complete with beds, table, cups and saucers, etc. There was a pint pot for father. I would lie on the 'bed' and 'sleep'. Clay came from 'diggings' and was only found now and then. At about eight years old, I made coffins out of clay, to play Flip, Flop, Floorbang! by hollowing them out and slapping them on the pavement.[3] As well as the boilers, the croft housed an amateur football pitch. The original goalposts were made from wooden struts bolted together, and were erected and dismantled every Saturday of the playing season. Later an improved version constructed of tubular metal was provided and left in place. It did not take the local children long to reshape the top bar by leaping up and hanging from the centre and other monkey-like antics. Whether this resulted in a lower goal average I never heard. In any case, I was never tall enough nor agile enough to leap up and hang from the crossbar, and so did not take a lot of interest.

The main attraction of this area to the younger fraternity, apart from the rides on the barges, was a line of stout fencing serving no particular purpose, of which the top rail was triangular in section. I could never walk along this myself, but most of my friends could. They jumped and ran, as well as standing on one leg and waving their arms in would-be graceful attitudes, pretending to be ballet dancers. This was not easy, as they were balancing on the apex of a triangle. As I was no great athlete, and afraid of heights, I had to be content with tippling over.

The park offered a variety of attractions, the most highly valued being the swings. In fact, the presence of swings was what stamped the place as a park. In our eyes, when we were old enough to explore other parts of Manchester in the school holidays, any place with swings was a park to us, even if it was only a 'red rec'.[4] I must say our arrival at these foreign venues was not welcomed, especially when there were queues for the helter-skelter and the wedding cake, or if we outsiders occupied any piece of equipment exclusively. It never actually came to blows, but 'Go and play in your own park', spoken in threatening terms, was not the worst thing we heard. Naturally we paid no heed.

The outdoor pleasures of children in spring and early summer, as is commonly the case, appeared and disappeared in a mysterious way. No one ever knew what prompted the first boy to fly his kite on the croft, or to whip a top along the pavement, causing the whole neighbourhood to erupt with kites and tops. Similarly with alleys and marbles. One moment the gutters were free of kneeling boys, next minute there were half a dozen small groups fiercely contending for the highly rated glassiest marbles, their pockets filling and emptying over and over.

Girls were more consistent. Skipping and ball-bouncing games, hopscotch and singing games were all-season pleasures, as long as the weather was halfway decent. We did covet, and obtain if we could, the exciting gars [hoops], which did have a limited season. These we would speed along the pavements and annoy passers-by. More usually we got cane hoops off barrels from the grocers, but these were much inferior to the metal ones with a ring and bar. The superior kind were very much envied and were gloried in when borrowed, a rare privilege only attainable if you were well in with a child from a better-off family. The class divisions always showed up in these seasonal pursuits: large, shop-bought kites, whips with leather thongs, immaculate new balls of string for those who could afford them. The rest of us shared a penny packet of tissue paper made with flour-and-water paste, and knotted together any oddments of string we could find. None of this make-do-and-mend spoiled our pleasure in the least.

Adults seldom went to the park unless as courting couples, and parks tended to close fairly early. Mostly, children were sent to play in the park with a bottle of water and a penny for lemonade crystals. In a group, this always led to arguments about what flavour to buy. My own choice was rainbow, but others preferred red, yellow, green or orange. The paddling pool was always crowded in the hot weather. Children often emerged with cut feet. Careful mothers urged their children to keep away from the pool for this reason, but it was difficult to resist.

The bookie's house, the end one of the garden houses, offered endless play opportunities in the shape of a 'dead wall'. This windowless wall was ideal for Two Ball, fancy versions of One Two Three Alaira,[5] assorted handstands and other gymnastic achievements.

There seemed to be a difference between the games we played in the street and the schoolyard variety. The latter were usually chasing and hiding games like Ralivo, and were more popular at playtime, along with group skipping and competitive ball-bouncing activities. Occasional bouts of sprinting took place in the street, but anything too organized was vetoed as too much like school. This did not apply to my little group of 'Dunces', who were usually

assembled near the men's clubhouse which adjoined our
playground. I once bought a packet of Virginia stock to sow
on the croft (all cinders) but no wonderful flowers came up.

## Nellie's Jokes and Sayings

Do not pass behind this car until you know the road is clean.
What is a good square meal? An Oxo cube [usually
    'cubby'].
How's your father's bald head? Same as I left it, in bed.
Where's your grammar? In bed with my grandpa.
Too many wells make a river, and you in the middle make it
    a bit bigger [in answer to 'well' as a protest to something].
Where's that (h)ammer? What 'ammer? A fool! [then rush
    off].
Take that grin off your face, or you'll laugh on the other
    side of your face in a minute. [These last two were
    followed by appropriate gestures, once out of sight.]
You'll see the devil if you keep looking in that glass.
Wait and see, like Asquith said.
Remember, you are forming your characters.
Don't let me interrupt your train of thought. [Reply:] Puff-
    puff.
When will you see a man with as many noses as there are
    days in the year? New Year's Day.
How long is a piece of string? Twice as long as half its
    length.
How many beans make five? One and another and two and
    a tother.
Well, it's a buggeroo [good tempered exasperation].
Come on, buggalugs [to a mischievous child, not in anger].
Step on a nick, you'll marry a brick, and a beetle will come
    to your wedding.
Neither sight nor light [of him].

# 5

# Food, Glorious Food

Nellie never starved, but she was often hungry. Children of the day were always on the lookout for extra food and treats. Getting the top of their father's breakfast boiled egg was a privilege enjoyed each day in turn by the six Mape children.

How to qualify for the maximum number of Sunday school 'treats' exercised the minds of the Empire Street youngsters. That was one way of getting something special to eat and drink. Going to the chip shop for her sister's tea gave Nellie the chance to pinch a few chips. Some mothers took their children cocoa and biscuits to eat at playtime, and at midday the workmen at the various factories in Gibbon Street were solicited for something from their lunches. Misshapes from the local sweet factory and Grice's twopenny bags were a regular source of sweets and cakes.

In later life, Nellie noted the foods that were common in her childhood: butter beans, plate meat pie, cabbage water, corned beef (at 2*d* a quarter), roast beef, boiled mutton, salmon and beef pastes, fat ducks, green peas and new potatoes. Savoury ducks and chitterlings were bought from the pork shop run by a German family. She was told that their windows had been broken during the First World War. A 'relish' (sauce or pickle) was usually called 'a bit of a relish', but what she meant by 'swaggering dicks', 'everlasting strips', 'port-wine sticks' and 'lucky horseshoes', I have no idea. As a child, Nellie thought that Farley's Rusks was an infantile complaint. For some reason, sultanas were the cause of much mirth.

Nellie was 'a little fat girl' who dieted for most of her adult life. It may be that the need to eat what you could when you could as a child was something she could not shake off in adulthood. This is how and what Nellie ate as a child.

I went hungry on most schooldays, but did not mention it at home. I was always worrying that I would get into trouble about these dinners, as there were very few pernickety children round those long trestle tables. However, it was not difficult to find a willing clearer-up. The few big tough lads among these under-14-year-old diners were very popular with the dinner ladies, who seemed to us to be very posh and very powerful.

One lad in particular, known to us as Gobbler, was able to accept offerings of food from other children even after three official plates of pudding. You were not supposed to leave any food, nor to take anything out of the room with you, so you had to be crafty in innumerable ways to avoid trouble. Gobbler was my saviour more than once, although he never charged for his services, unlike the obliging little girl who ate my stewed tripe every Thursday when I was in a convalescent home at six years of age.

At some stage in my later years at school, free school dinners came into my life. There were no other school dinners available, apart from these for necessitous children. The food was served originally in a large hall at the local police station, and later transferred to the nearby Methodist chapel. The meals never altered. Everyone hated the bread, already cut into quarter slices, of pepper-and-salt appearance and neither brown nor white. It was very nutritious, no doubt, but did not resemble the white, factory-made bread we were used to. It was more like sawdust! Some days there would be a very thick soup with lots of haricot beans.

There was usually a pudding: ginger, currant, etc. This arrived in huge metal trays, and was cut into squares and served with custard. Whatever the variety, it left a coating of grease in the mouth for hours afterwards. Potato pie came in similar containers, and seemed to me to have more of the peculiar smell which all the cooked meat dishes seemed to have. I usually ate only the crust. Some days, knowing what would be on offer, I just did not go, hoping my absence would not be noticed and reported at home. I always went on Fridays, because this was cheese and apple day, although the bread for the sandwiches was dry. Your apple would be cut in half, to make sure you ate it then and there, and to prevent you giving it away or selling it, but this rule was almost totally ignored. To most children, there was no such thing as unpopular food.

I was not a fussy eater at home. I had not yet come into contact with families where food was offered of a type that was disliked. Therefore, no such episodes of uneaten food being saved from one meal to another ever occurred in our house. It would have seemed nonsensical to me in those days to offer items likely to be refused. I imagined that a family menu, such as our own, evolved naturally from a consensus of acceptable items. This covered a somewhat restricted range, but avoided waste and mealtime scenes, besides fitting in with the narrow means available.

Generally, people could only speak with confidence about their own eating habits, as meals were eaten behind closed doors. It was not considered correct to call at mealtimes, and apologies were always offered if this happened accidentally.

Occasionally, critical items of gossip leaked out, such as a family where the mother 'lowenced them out', i.e. rigidly adhered to preset portions, irrespective of mitigating circumstances. A number of the Empire Street housewives clung with pathetic pride to the vow that they never had, and never would, subject their families to this last humili- ation, as they saw it, although the customary constraints of a poverty-line income amounted to much the same thing.

It was not good manners to talk at the table, and children often stood to eat their meals. A chair at the table was part of the rites of passage to adulthood (wage-earning) in many families. Portions of food may have differed in size, but for adults to have denied items of food to the children was not something you would like the neighbours to know – such as the quarter pound of 'best butter' clandestinely enjoyed by even the best of mothers in many cases. The boiled egg for father was legitimised by cutting off a fairly generous top to be given to each child in turn, and which was eagerly awaited. That this practice was fairly widespread was confirmed by the show-off mother who called her daughter in for tea with the frequent loud invitation to 'Come in and 'ave a wole [*sic*] egg'!

Some families watered the pot [of tea] for the children when the parents had finished. Cabbage water was thought to be good for children. Jam was bought on a saucer at a penny a time, scooped out from an enormous stone jar at the corner grocer's. This was known as 'a relish'. I never heard of people having jam and butter (marge in our case) on bread. All except the smallest members of the family put together their own butties. Contrary to the assertions of the ignorant, a sandwich is not a butty. A kind neighbour made us children little treats, such as on one occasion a summer pudding. (Could she have been in service, I wonder?) She could never understand the requirement to fast before Holy Communion and liked to give me a little something 'for after' in my pocket.

Some children were allowed to join their mothers at lunchtime during school holidays. With my mother working at the mill, when I was younger I was allowed to go there for my dinner in the holidays. One of my great pleasures was to climb the outside staircase at the mill and brew up for my mother and her workmates in the dinner hour. I can still feel the half-round brass knob you pushed in to get boiling water; I loved it. Brewing up at the constant-boiling-water tap was a great treat. The mill was also very warm, another bonus in the winter.

Most kids were perpetually hungry. At lunchtime, we children would gather round the factory gates in our street. 'Any lunches?' was the cry. Some of the factory hands would save us part of their lunches. If you were lucky, it would be an apple or a cake. We were even introduced to mustard. More usually, we were given dried-up sandwiches. If so, most children just ate the meat or cheese filling. It never seemed to us children that this was deliberate, although many of the workers had their favourites. All the factories in our street were fair game, although we didn't have much to do with the rubber works, except at Christmas, because it wasn't at our end of the row of houses. The African factory was even more out of our world, being round a dog's-leg bend.

One of the benefits of becoming a worker and bringing home a wage was that some more junior member of the family had to fetch your tea from the local emporium, known as 'the chippy'. Chip shops were open till midnight 'of a pastime' (Easter, Whit, Bank Holidays). I was never a tall person, even when fully grown, and I missed going on the chip-shop errands when promoted as above, because I had only just got used to being able to look over the high serving counter without having to mountaineer up the skirting board. You only got a favourable reply to your request for 'Any scratchings?' if they could see you. The younger members thus conscripted into chip-shop duty soon learned to ask for a few scratchings. Scratchings – scraps of cooked batter served out of the hot fat – were never refused to regular customers.

It was a rite of passage to adulthood when somebody else went for your tea. One disadvantage was the loss of those few stolen chips filched from the paper-covered basin on the way home. Square in section and deliciously tasty and brown, they have never been equalled. They were particularly appreciated on cold winter evenings when the fiat went forth to 'Fetch your sister's tea from the chip shop.' Depending on the economic state of the household on any particular day, a choice beyond the usual chips and peas might be given. I always plumped for scallops – thick potato slices cooked in batter – knowing full well that this would deprive the messenger of the few delicious chips usually prised from under the newspaper cover of the basin, during the brief journey home, since to break off a bit of one of the scallops was out of the question. I was amused by a notice in the chip shop: 'Please do not ask for credit, as a refusal often offends.' Doesn't it always?

The toffee works, besides its delicious smell, kept a box the size of a tea chest in the entrance hall under the eye of the manager. This contained less than perfect items – kalis, lollipops, etc. Many and varied were the theories advanced among us kids as to the purpose of this box. One, which was dismissed as ridiculous, was that the workers were allowed to take a handful home for the family as they clocked off, perhaps every Friday. Whatever was intended, practice proved that any child not too tall, or else suitably bent over, was 'never noticed' by the otherwise vigilant supervisor, as long as only one item was taken. Believable or otherwise, the theory worked, given due observation of the unspoken 'one item per child' rule. Nothing was said if you put your hand into the tub and took just one item. It might be anything: toffee, tobacco, a lucky turnover or a sugar pig.

It still remains a mystery to me all these years later how a large bakery firm came to have so many leftover cakes at the end of the week – not every week, presumably, but every so often, when word got round via those in the know, that a limited number of Grice's twopenny bags would be available on the following Saturday. A small select group of Empire Streeters would be rounded up, though never more than one from the same family. I can't remember, at this distance of time, whether this was a company rule to ensure fair distribution, but at the time I put it down as a natural precaution to deal with the inevitable domestic inquisition.

'Funny how they never give you a vanilla', was often the comment as the mothers inspected the contents on our return. We didn't dare take more than one item out of each bag. Some children went for quantity rather than quality, choosing the largest bun of the lot, but the pinnacle of desire was a vanilla slice, a luxury which never came our way in ordinary life, not even as a Christmas treat. This was not surprising, as vanillas cost 2*d* each against the usual halfpenny for a fairy cake or a penny for an iced fancy cake. Long experience told the organizers of such treats that arguments, if nothing more serious, would be the inevitable result if these crown jewels of the cake world were included in the share-out along with the more mundane iced fingers and Bakewell tarts.

All this came flooding back to me some thirty years later. I was a novice volunteer helper at a pensioners' Christmas party in a small Lancashire town. My task was to assemble and set out a tasteful selection of cakes on large plates down the centre of the long trestle tables with instructions to 'make them look nice'. Delighted with this high-profile task, I went in for a variety of patterns and worked away unsupervised until just before kick-off, when there came a desperate shriek which called me back to duty. 'Every plate must be the same, and every plate must have a vanilla!' I suffered contemptuous glances from the experienced ladies keeping guard on the door until the plates were put right. I was then conscripted for kitchen duty right away, so was not present at 'cake time', leaving me with the mystery of

'Who got the vanilla?' out of each group of six, and how they managed it. I did essay a feeble enquiry during washing-up, but apparently, to the experienced ladies drying up at breakneck speed, it was 'no contest'.

My abiding recollection of this sort of occasion from my youth was the tragic error of the extra cream cake. The two hard-working and devoted ladies who had organised the tea had provided one fancy cake for each child. I think the occasion must have been the crowning of the Rechabite Queen, because we did not always have a tea party. A plentiful tea was provided, the two adults in charge pressing us to take another sandwich and another cup of tea. The final treat was a large platter of fresh cream cakes, from which we all chose one. After we had all chosen and eaten our cakes, and when everyone seemed to have finished, one of the genteel ladies in charge picked up the plate with two cakes still remaining and offered them all round the table. Coaxingly, she asked, 'Can't anyone manage another of these delicious cakes?'

Nobody offered until it came to me. As the plate passed in front of me, I reached out and took a cream puff. I knew the minute I touched it that I had misjudged the situation. I immediately realised that this was a gross error – it was written all over the other faces round the table. The others knew that the invitation was only manners and not to be taken seriously, but I did not. Having handled the cake, there was no going back, and the delicious cream puff was eaten, with great difficulty, during a frozen silence. That cream puff nearly choked me, and I still don't know how I got it down.

This was the first time I had caught an adult saying what they did not mean. I later worked out – two ladies, two buns – that they were to have their tea later. They ought to have kept back the two extra cakes, but reviewing the mysterious rules of etiquette, especially those attached to eating and drinking, I decided that correct observance required the complete assortment of cakes to be offered initially. This was one of life's little lessons for me, which I never forgot. In my world, no one would offer something, food or anything else, that you weren't expected to take. On the other hand, there were social hypocrisies – for instance, all children we minded for other people were reported as having been 'good as gold', even if they had screamed the whole time.

Christmas and birthday parties were much looked forward to for the food and the (non-alcoholic) drink. There would be large bottles of assorted minerals from the corner shop: Vimto, Dandelion & Burdock and the like. The refreshments would very likely be potted-meat sandwiches, jelly and custard, biscuits and cake. We usually got an Easter egg of some sort, however small, and always some of the clay-coloured chocolate which showed up again at Christmas in selection boxes and 'smokers' outfits' – sweets and chocolates made to look like cigarettes, cigars and pipes.

I remember my first introduction to tinned sliced peaches and Carnation milk when I was about twelve. It happened when I was asked to accompany a better-off young cousin, an only child, to a birthday party some distance from Empire Street. What an eye-opener it was – the food, the clothes, the comfortable furniture – although the home itself was only an ordinary terraced working-class house. Sixty years later, the special pleasure of tinned sliced peaches and evaporated milk still overtops even fresh fruit and real cream because of its association with that childhood memory.

## Dieting

Nellie dieted for most of her adult life. In 1967, 47-year-old Nellie joined the Manchester Dance Circle, in her own words, 'to try to preserve some semblance of physical fitness'. This was Nellie's diet in 1953, as dictated by her doctor:

Do not drink more than half a pint of milk per day. Reduce fluid to two pints unless otherwise ordered.

BREAKFAST
Fresh or cooked fruit without sugar. One ounce of bread thinly buttered. Tea or coffee (no sugar).

MIDDAY MEAL
Tomato juice or orange juice or melon. Average helping of lean meat or fish or liver. Green vegetables (unlimited quantity). Average helping of carrots, peas, beans. Fresh fruit or stewed fruit without sugar. Biscuit and cheese or small portion of custard or fruit, or approx. half an average helping of sweet.

TEA
Meat or fish or liver or tripe or eggs or cheese. Green salad with tomato and half an egg. One round thin bread and butter. Raw or cooked fruit (no sugar). Tea or coffee (not all milk).

SUPPER
Cup of tea and one sweet biscuit.

# 6

# *Seasonal Joys*

There was always something to look forward to in Gibbon Street. Each season of the year brought its own particular delights. Some traditions are still with us. Some, like the Whit Walks, are much diminished, while others were special to the locality. It is a truism to say that people in those days made their own amusements, but to the young Nellie this was a major part of life. There was no television. While some people did have radios, Nellie never mentions having one in her house. There was the cinema, the theatre and several regular fairs, but throughout the year the local community celebrated with its own entertainments and traditions.

In my own childhood in the 1940s and 1950s, the Whit Walks were still a hugely important tradition. All kinds of organisations took part, not just churches and Sunday schools. In Bury, the processions would gather at a suitable piece of open ground just outside the town a good hour or more before kick-off. Then we would process through the town centre, with massive crowds all the way. Money was regularly thrown to us children, but woe betide any other youngster who grabbed cash thrown by a doting parent to their child. 'That's my money!' I was often told as I picked up a coin, especially if it was silver instead of the usual copper. You had to comply, or risk the wrath of a vengeful parent emerging from the side of the road.

Walking with my Sunday school (I defied my atheistic parents and got myself baptised at fourteen) it was a much sought-after honour to 'carry the banner'. Just to hold one of the ribbons attached to the banner was a much fought-over position. To be one of the two big lads bearing the weight of the carrying poles was the highest role I could aspire to. With these coveted positions invariably going to teachers' pets or to children whose parents had influence in the church, I had no chance. 'Next year, perhaps', was all the consolation I could get. But I did have my moment of glory. Elected leader of my senior scout troop (yes, elected by my fellow scouts), I had the honour of being right at the head of the Bury Whit Monday Parade.

Our scout troup, curiously named the 44th Bury despite being the first such troop to be formed in the town, was attached to Bury's main Church of England church and was known as the BOHOTS (Bishop of Hulme's Own Troop). 'Just be glad we were not, as originally intended, called the Rector of Bury's Own Troop, the ROBOTS,' said my scoutmaster. We were the senior organisation in the church, so we fronted the parade and I was first off. Of course, proudly carrying the flag in the prescribed manner, arm crooked at nose height, I was unable to collect any cash. But it was well worth the sacrifice.

Being dark-haired, I carried out the New Year tradition as a teenager as the first caller for my parents and grandparents, and also in my early married life for my own family (the significance of dark hair will become clear in Nellie's account). But other traditions described by my mother were not continued. Nellie very much wanted to keep herself to herself and discouraged visitors. Yet her own childhood had been full of social interaction.

Like the posh people in the stories I used to read, we had our own 'season', or rather a whole list of seasonal pleasures to look forward to. We liked to make the most of them, just as much as those higher up in the social scale. Easter, Whitsuntide, August Bank Holiday, Christmas and New Year were known as 'pastimes'. Things had to be very bad indeed for these to be allowed to pass without some acknowledgement of their importance in the yearly calendar. A more informal event, referred to as 'a bit of a collocation', was almost as much a social duty as a pastime. 'Keeping it up' was the usual reference to social gatherings. My father's 7 p.m. bedtime edict kept most of the adult evening activities out of our reach. When, occasionally, permission was given to 'stop on' for the fireworks or pageant – oh, what bliss!

To deal with pastimes chronologically, I begin with 1st January. For this, we must go back to the last few minutes of the old year, when an unnatural silence enveloped Empire Street and its immediate neighbourhood. Everyone held their breath, with no wireless or gramophone to be heard. All the women and girls were indoors, tense and expectant, while the big lads and the men congregated on the croft, a piece of open ground next to the mill and the boiler works.

On the stroke of midnight, the silence was shattered by a thunderous tattoo on the boilers stored on the croft, awaiting repair. Every possible weapon was used, from sledgehammers to broken bricks. Without this ear-splitting annual ceremony, we could scarcely have imagined that the New Year had really begun. This performance was much enjoyed and was a source of local pride. To be present at this late hour was one of the rites of adulthood in our area. Using actual hammers was usually restricted to heads of households or their substitutes. Lesser males had to make do with pokers, bricks or a piece of wood. This annual event was known as 't' knockin on't boilers'.

The banging ceremony couldn't be allowed to last too long, because all the dark-haired 'knockers' had to hurry away, with coal in pocket. They had to let the New Year in for their own families, and for their ginger and grey-haired neighbours. It was traditional on New Year's Eve for a dark-haired man, with a piece of coal, to thrust in at the front door. This ritual involved a mop or sweeping brush made up to look like some hideous heathen idol, a pirate skull, or an overpainted 'Red Indian' complete with feathered headdress. All the dark-haired men in the street were booked well ahead to let the New Year in, although some people disregarded this custom. It was correct to scream and pretend to faint at the sight of this intruder before joining in the traditional potato pie supper in one of the houses.

At New Year an invitation to the annual hotpot supper was given. The correct repast to offer guests was potato pie, usually made in an enamel washing-up bowl to accommodate the large numbers of guests. Invitees took their own plate or dish, and usually a spoon, and a good time was had by all. Our end of Empire Street was in the capable hands of Aunt Dolly (in reality a cousin). With the hotpot bubbling in the oven, all the people from our end went back into their own houses, closed the door and remained silent. This quiet gathering enjoyed card games and a few drinks. They were waiting for Dolly's own New Year's Eve ritual, which happened during the day or evening and which she never missed. Each year she dressed up a sweeping brush or a Turk's head whitewash brush in the most hideous, hair-raising style imaginable. One year it was a Red Indian, another a skeleton, and neither the make-up nor the headdress were spared.

Aunt Dolly could always be relied on to keep the party going. Earlier on New Year's Eve, she would visit all the houses at our end, confronting each 'frightened' household with this hideous figure. One yell from Dolly, followed by 'Hotpot's ready, everybody welcome', and she proceeded to the next house. As soon as some of us were old enough to give unwanted advice to our mothers, we learned that there was often competition to answer the door on these occasions, and to put on the best show of 'fear'.

The next seasonal milestone was Easter, with usually at least one travelling fair setting up locally. The most important day in Empire Street was Good Friday. I wouldn't have missed the Good Friday outing for anything, in spite of the early start, the long walk and the uncomfortable recollection of our teacher's pre-holiday urging. We were told to regard Good Friday as a day of sadness, and to save any thought of enjoyment until Easter Sunday. These references to the 'real meaning' of Good Friday from our teachers were totally disregarded.

Easter was a joy, as much in the anticipation as the realisation. There was the holiday from school, Easter eggs and the annual trip to Daisy Nook, a popular beauty spot some miles away. I went to Daisy Nook on Good Friday as soon as I was old enough to walk the distance. Daisy Nook itself, a small area of country sandwiched between industrial districts on the east side of Manchester, and now fortunately a country park, was a good distance from Empire Street. This limited the annual group to those old enough to walk so far. However, we could usually muster ten or a dozen.

There was always a fair, with rides and sideshows, music entertainers and cheapjacks (stallholders with their distinctive selling patter). Everybody of a suitable age – young, that is to say – went to Daisy Nook on Good Friday. We expected, and got, better than usual refreshments. There was always a hard-boiled egg each, special to the day, and the inevitable slice of yellow shop cake. In my family we also had my mother's Good Friday speciality: salmon sandwiches with a home-made sandwich spread made with real tinned salmon, not with the usual twopence-a-quarter salmon paste from the corner shop. There were similar supplies for our day trips to the seaside, with the added bonus of sand on the sandwiches!

Mothers usually insisted on a senior girl leading the group, even if one of our older cousins had to be recruited (and bribed) from several streets away. If there were two of them, as was the usual custom, we could count on them disappearing soon after we arrived to follow their own teenage inclinations. That left us younger children free to paddle in the freezing-cold river, to shriek on the swing boats and generally make nuisances of ourselves round the sideshows.

There were the cheapjacks selling fake gold watches, the conjuror apparently drilling into a boy's skull and filling a glass with milk from there, and the other annual marvels of the Daisy Nook Easter Fair. We loved it all: the blaring steam organ, the dobby-horses, the customary fairground eatables, especially the black peas, and the whole jolly hustle and bustle which said to us that winter was over and spring was really here.

One particular Good Friday has stayed in my memory. On this occasion, when I was about twelve, we were a largish mixed group of youngsters. There were two older girls in charge, as laid down by our cautious parents. These two went their own way once we had arrived, and the rest of us went paddling in the ice-cold river. Tiring of this, we opted to eat our packed lunches, to get our strength up for the rest of the entertainment. Two somewhat older boys, brothers of about twelve to thirteen years of age, had asked if they could come with us. We had been a bit doubtful about including them because we didn't know them very well. They had been 'put away' for some youthful misdoings and had only just returned home – but still we agreed. We made for the water right away, and, after this senseless, freezing splashing about, we were more than ready to open our lunches. We all got our sandwiches out. I knew what mine would include: the special hard-boiled egg, the slice of shop cake, and salmon sandwiches with mother's home-made sandwich spread.

We had two ordinary lads with us, as well as the two rather rough lads, and one nicely mannered boy, Roy, who was somebody's cousin. Roy came up to Fred, the nearest of our 'ordinary' lads, and whispered something in his ear. Fred looked a bit nonplussed for a moment. Then, looking into his lunch packet, he called out in a loud voice, 'Ugh! Cheese sandwiches again! Can anybody eat one?' I did not see any gestures or silent signals, but after a brief pause Joe and Alf, the two 'rough' lads who had tacked themselves onto us, each accepted a sandwich. The other children caught on as if by magic, offering 'unwanted' items from their own supplies. The girls added biscuits and cake, and even I did as I caught on belatedly. One of life's little lessons?

The explanation, passed on as opportunity allowed later during the afternoon, was that Roy had seen the brothers unwrap their lunch. The two big boys were found to have nothing but bread and marge, or 'bread and spit' in male talk. Thanks to Roy and Fred, we gained the unspoken resolve to offer the two rough boys some of the more exciting sandwiches available among the lunches of the other boys and girls, without hurting their feelings or risking a rebuff. With exquisite and quite unexpected tact, one after another of us twigged what was going on. We each pretended to be full up, or fed up of cheese, or egg, or meat paste. It worked like a charm, as Joe and Alf 'offered' to eat up the supposed leftovers.

I wondered if Roy had noticed this on the way there. I knew I would never have been quick enough to respond as Fred had done. How I envied him! We were all agreed that Joe and Alf would probably get a 'good leathering' when they got home, because they nearly always did, whatever their behaviour. Their dad was noted for it. We had a good day out before making our way home, somewhat tired.

On Good Friday, the big day of the year, we all had a little spending money, but it did not run to sideshows. After I started work, I did attend a similar fair with a group of workmates. We daringly paid our sixpences for 'Paris With The Lid Off', having been promised beautiful ladies 'wearing nothing but a smile'. Needless to say, the little group of females (hardly 'girls' by any standards), wearing tawdry costumes and swinging tired arms and legs, was a big let-down. We were hustled out without a by-your-leave.

The remainder of the Easter Weekend was nothing special. For most of us there was the cinema on Saturday with a penny for the pictures and a halfpenny for sweets. We got our Easter eggs on Sunday, comparing price and size with street friends. As I remember them, the chocolate eggs we got then were much inferior to anything you could buy now. The colour was insipid and the flavour nowhere near the occasional taste of 'Cabbries' (Cadbury's) gleaned from friends with generous uncles.

On Monday we usually went to the park, as nobody felt equal to another long walk after Friday. Easter Monday in the park held a number of possibilities. The swings might be chained up, as they were on Sundays, but the paddling pool was available, and there was plenty of room for chasing games, as long as a good-tempered 'parky' happened to be on duty. Sometimes a Sunday school group would be there for sports, and occasionally a warm-hearted vicar would rope in some of us for the odd race to make up the numbers. Even if he didn't, there were sure to be sack and egg-and-spoon races. We could watch the fun and jeer at the losers. We could always find something to enjoy, though nothing matched up to Good Friday at Daisy Nook.

Seven weeks after Easter came Whit Week, but before this almost every little neighbourhood had its own May Queen. Empire Street was no exception. A lot of thought and a lot of work went into the organisation of this annual event, though the programme was much the same year after year. First choose your Queen. The basic requirement was for a girl in the seven-year-old bracket, with a pretty face and curly hair if available. The May Queen played a major part in the annual May crowning in church. We followed this tradition in our own street enactment of a May ceremony.

The May Queen required access to a long dress, and a lace curtain for her train. My ambition was to make all the costumes of crêpe paper, but this needed venture capital not usually available. We made do with tissue paper, of which you got a lot of different colours for a penny. With this we decorated a half-hoop of the ever-useful cane from the grocery barrels, to make a garland (absolutely essential) for the two Maids of Honour to hold over the Queen. They were dressed in Empire-style dresses, which I considered extremely frumpish. There was a pianist, a jester, another boy who was some sort of courtier, and four 'national' dancers, of whom I was one (Welsh). Our May Queen wore a lace-curtain veil. This was easily obtained, as everyone had lace curtains.

Some groups contained a cowboy or a Red Cross nurse, depending on what costumes were available. Occasionally there would be a miniature maypole. Five or six shillings would be collected at the doors, and this would result in a marvellous party for up to a dozen kids. The tea party, which was the real object of the exercise, took place in our backyard. The comestibles were paid for from the contents of the collecting tin. The party fare was all decided on and prepared by the members of the 'cast', to everyone's satisfaction (as a rule). Brown bread was essential, and red jelly. The Rechabites [see Chapter 7] held a tea party for the crowning of the Queen. The Queen and court consisted of the Queen herself, her little sister, who played the Maid of Honour, and two bigger girls who were also Maids of Honour.

We sang our May Queen song, in which we 'merrily claimed the day', adding a few simple jig steps when we came to 'Dance, dance so merrily'. We finished up with 'Little Brown Jug' and 'Three Little Maids From Japan' – a favourite number. A strange mixture, but that's what we sang.

### THE MAY QUEEN SONG

In gentle Janey Thomas
We crown the Queen of May
With hearts and voices singing
We merrily claim the day
The Queen of May is here today
To give us all a holiday
Dance, dance so merrily
Sing, sing so cheerily
No one can dance so gay as we
Singing so merrily all the day.

Whitsuntide generated more excitement than any part of Easter apart from Good Friday. New clothes were essential on Whit Sunday. Even the poorest families made some attempt to conform with this tradition. However, in large families 'new' seldom meant previously unworn, either by the current wearer or one or more predecessors. For one thing, the preparations, the getting together of sufficient new-looking clothing to make a good show on Whit Sunday morning, were spread over a long period. In a household where there was a man's wage coming in, or with several adult children willing to stump up a few bob for the younger ones, things were not so difficult. For the rest of us, money had to be found to get white dresses out of pawn, clothing cheques had to be applied for, and reliable second-hand dealers and market stalls needed to be kept an eye on. There were plenty of itinerant vendors, enticing the juvenile populace with balloons and whirling windmills to 'bring out your rags', but we saved our 'decent rags' for a fellow religionist who came only down the back entry. This was for respectable privacy, not for concealment.

On Whit Sunday morning we showed ourselves in our Whit Week clothes to relatives and well-disposed neighbours. This was not very exciting, but the customary three-pences and sixpences which found their way into our pockets made it all worth the effort. In the afternoon, still togged up, we could watch the smaller Sunday schools and chapels as they processed in pretty dresses and Fauntleroy suits round their immediate neighbourhoods, but these were minor affairs compared with the major walks.

It was Monday for the Church of England, Friday for the Catholics.[1] These processions were glorious and heart-lifting sights with banners flying and bands playing all the way to the city centre. There was a great deal of good-natured rivalry between the spectators of the two big processions according to where their religious loyalties lay, especially in those years when Monday was fine and Friday wet, or vice versa. There were cries of 'God knows his own' from either party as appropriate, and boozy choruses of 'Sons of the Sea', or anything with an Irish flavour, as the day went on and the jollifications gathered strength.

The Italian community held their own procession. This was a magnificent show in national costume, with a statue of Our Lady carried along in a sea of Madonna lilies. The atmosphere was entirely different, and the seriousness of the whole occasion seemed to spill over into the people lining the streets. This made the visit to 'watch the Italians walk' a very moving experience. The custom of paying public honour to the Virgin Mary has a long history. During the Middle Ages, England was spoken of as 'Our Lady's Dowry', and the Holy Virgin was widely revered as the embodiment of every womanly virtue. Most Catholic churches continued this tradition on the first Sunday in May (Mary's own month) with a simple, much-loved and moving ceremony. This involved the chosen child placing a crown of flowers on the statue of 'The Queen of Heaven', to the accompaniment of hymns in her praise.

Summer saw the Co-operative Society annual carnival. I would go with some of my cousins with tickets bought by our Uncle Tom. The carnival was held in a field with sports and games. There were the same refreshments every time, including a chocolate horseshoe.

Christmas was the best time for getting in on the largesse so recklessly offered by various Sunday and ragged schools. How this calendar of opportunities became known to the initiated still remains a mystery. The big-hearted family of girls who were the core of Empire Street life could not only supply the dates of at least two non-clashing 'Christmas breakfasts', but also how many weeks of previous attendance were needed to qualify for the treat. We somehow managed to attend five Sunday schools of the mission type in order to qualify for summer treats. It never occurred to any of us that the ladies who ran these affairs were well aware of the significance of these seasonal influxes and probably considered that even six weeks of contact would be beneficial.

Occasionally one would come across a Sunday school treat with races and games. These always seemed to be run by jolly, amiable clergymen and well-dressed lady helpers who would rope in any stray children to take part, irrespective of entitlement. All the local children knew quite well how to stand around in such a way as to be invited to join in the organised games. This did not always find favour with the legitimate runners. The 'legal' Sunday schoolers made no protest, unless one of the interlopers won. This was a tactical mistake which could lead to much unpleasantness, and loss of profits. It was not unknown for the small prizes to change hands under pressure when the eyes of authority were momentarily elsewhere. Once out of range of the managing authorities, there would be the retrieval of ill-gotten gains by the superior numbers of legitimate competitors.

There was great excitement when the word went round that the shop windows had been dressed for Christmas. We children went in a group, each child competing to be the first to claim a bike, a doll's cot or pram, with a breathless 'I'm having that' – a claim that was never disputed. There was always another evening, in fact many more during the pre-Christmas shopping season, in which we could indulge this heady fantasizing. There was much disappointed groaning as the gorgeous display gradually thinned out and favourite items disappeared. Opposite the Co-op was a shoe shop with right-angled plate-glass windows, just made for the old game of raising one arm and one leg while appearing (like comedian Harry Worth) to float on air. This provided many a hilarious interval between the big toy-worshipping sessions, especially if you could work out a particularly effective floating-on-air display.

We were never allowed inside the rubber works in Empire Street, but we did very well out of their Christmas do. The workers would hand out bottles of pop ad lib. Eventually, a man would come to the door and say 'Come in, you kids, and finish off.' There was coloured paper round the lampshades, beautiful and bright. The men smelled of beer, but there was plenty of food. Kids from other streets were kept out by the doorman.

All Christmas chocolate items, smoker's outfits, selection boxes and the like seemed to be available only in a second-grade, claylike confection – even the block chocolate sold by the quarter pound. We never thought of criticising, being only too glad to get any at all. Then it was New Year's Eve, and the yearly round of pastimes would start again.

As well as visits to the local park, there were other possibilities for longer forays. For example, the River Medlock and the adjoining sandhills were just beyond the park. There we could paddle, catch jacksharps [tiddlers], and slide down the railway banking on any convenient piece of wood or cardboard. There was the paddling pool and the swings. On occasion there would be games of netball and even dancing round the bandstand. We thrilled each other with horror stories of the smallpox hospital which used to stand there, explaining to each other how the dead bodies were floated down the river after dark. 'They weren't allowed to bury them because of the infection,' someone would say. No one doubted the logic of this explanation at the time.

Full and varied as the locally available pleasures were, we did occasionally go further afield. Almost always this was on foot in juvenile groups and without the doubtful benefit of adult company. The exceptions to this were the 'treats' organized by official bodies, some to be paid for, others gratis, when transport was often laid on. We also had our own full-day visits to the country. Family outings were the exception rather than the rule. We did occasionally see groups of four parents and children in the local park, but the usual procedure was to send young children with an older sister.

Family parties could be found picnicking in our park at weekends, but these tended to be above the poverty level. They were 'posh' in our eyes, and given to the reckless habit of discarding empty mineral bottles in waste bins. These were worth at least a penny in deposit money, and many were worth twopence. Eagle-eyed lads quickly retrieved them in order to claim back the deposit. This needed finesse and know-how, as shopkeepers were very sharp to refuse 'other people's bottles'. There were ways round this problem – busy shops, short-sighted old ladies, and straightforward lying.

# The Demon Drink

Whatever organisation she belonged to, Nellie threw herself into its activities with great energy and commitment. Whether it was her school, the Young Communist League, or the Costume Society, Nellie gave herself totally to the cause. This is very apparent in her membership of the Juvenile Rechabites, the youth arm of this popular and highly influential temperance movement and welfare society. She remained an active member despite being told to terminate her membership by her Catholic head teacher. By the time she was seventeen, Nellie was quite ready to criticise the elders of the Independent Order of Rechabites, with its high officials sporting their decorative regalia, as 'old fossils' who needed to get up to date and work to turn the youth of the day away from alcohol. Nellie, a lifelong abstainer, had a lot to say about the 'demon drink'.

In his book, *Leisure, Gender and Culture in Salford & Manchester 1900–1939*, the author Andrew Davies writes that leisure for men was equated with pubs and drinking. It is extraordinary for me to read drinking constantly referred to as leisure or recreation. Davies considers that poverty is not caused by drinking, but is the cause of restrictions on the frequency and amount of drinking sessions. My own feelings as a non-drinker are that this is true, but it is a sad state of affairs. None of Davies's interviewees makes mention of officially provided clubs for unemployed men such as I remember in Philips Park.

I was never allowed out late enough at night to take advantage of this piece of social observation. Although, according to my father's rigid rule, we children had to be in bed by seven o'clock, an exception must have been made for the fortnightly Juvenile Rechabite meeting. Besides which, as I have mentioned, my father was frequently in hospital or in a convalescent home, when rules were somewhat more elastic. In my own childhood experience, I knew little about adult ways of spending their 'leisure' time. All I knew of pubs was that they were a suitable place to hang about for Guy Fawkes pennies. It was advisable to accost the customers coming out rather than going in, for obvious reasons.

Much boozing went on, naturally. As a rule there was no violence, only occasional outbreaks of street jollity. There were choruses of 'You Called Me Baby Doll' and the mystifying 'I Don't Care What Becomes of Me', which did not seem to have any further lyrics but apparently had a lot of meaning. One regular Saturday night performance in our neighbourhood involved a real Victorian-type melodrama. Picture the scene: a weeping mother, with her current baby in her arms, is thrown out into the street by her drunken husband, irrespective of the state of the weather. She, begging to be let in, is supported by various neighbours attempting to conciliate, all to no avail. He roars from behind the locked door, 'You're never going to come in no more.' Eventually, the local bobby arrives, presumably summoned, according to custom, as soon as the whole drama blows up. At the first word of legal authority, the door is meekly opened, the weeping mother and child are admitted, and no more is heard of it until the next Saturday. We children are 'up in the gods' in our bedrooms, so to speak, with not a very good view. We never knew the ins and outs or the rationale of all these goings-on, but you could pick up quite a lot in the corner shop on a Sunday morning.

There was always at least one neighbour who thought that the 'Humane Man', whoever he was, should have been sent for. And the fact that Mrs James was given to reading books, in this case paper novelettes, and had named one of her boys Jeremy and another Clarence, was held by many to be a contributing factor to these regular scenes.

Another case involved the Tomlinsons, a family of grown lads whose mother had been 'badly done to' by a drunken husband. There was a dramatic scene one cold winter's night when the old dad was thrown into the street in his shirt, minus his trousers. We had a grandstand view from our bedroom window, but were quickly made to come away. Our expressions of pity for the old chap were brushed to one side. 'You don't know what she's had to put with – he deserves worse than that', we were told.

The year 1935 was the centenary of the Rechabite movement. Nellie, then fifteen, had an article about the coming centenary celebrations published in the *Juvenile Rechabite* magazine in June, which is reproduced here:

'Oh, to be in England now that April's there', said the poet of good thought indeed, and if we could commend it to our own use it would read, 'Oh, to be in Belle Vue when the month of June is here', because at Belle Vue on a certain day in June there will be everything to delight the mind and eye of any Rechabite. In a word, the Centenary Celebrations. I am looking forward with keen delight and anticipation to everything connected with the celebrations. Firstly, the amusements, the many thrilling and amusing rides, and the boating. Also, the museum with the various exhibitions, some weird, some amusing, but all interesting.

Then I want to see the extremely varied and interesting collection of animals from all parts of the world. I want to see the fireworks, and I am longing to see the seven Temperance Queens crowned. I want to see the Temperance Bands, I want to see the Pageant, I want to hear the great Political Leader speak. How I am going to cram it all into a single day, I don't know, but I am longing with every fibre of my being for the month of June to come quickly, though it's no use – Father Time won't be hurried up.

I hope I shall meet a lot of people and hear many dialects, each so different from the other, and the people who speak them so scattered, but all united by the golden link of Rechabitism. One good thing I want to see which I have never seen before, and that is all the bars being closed so that no intoxicating liquors can be sold, and every drink either removed or camouflaged in some way.

Some are looking forward to the music, some to the fireworks. The spectacle and grandeur are anticipated by some, but there is one thing finer than all of these. I am looking forward to the celebrations, because in looking forward we can also look backward, back on the achievements of our forefathers, who bravely bore the banner of Temperance over obstacles well-nigh insurmountable, through severe trials and tribulations, through scorn and ridicule, with tireless faith and staunch courage, and have kept the torch of thrift and total abstinence burning brightly throughout the past century.

The Centenary Celebrations signify the culmination of all the efforts, and give us renewed zeal and energy to go forward spreading Truth and Temperance wherever we can. 'Until one great shout ascend. The world is free.' – Sister Nellie Mape, 'Hope of Bradford' Juvenile Tent No. 9, Manchester District No. 1.

In 1937, Nellie won the Rechabites' annual national essay-writing competition.[1] The subject was 'Alcohol, Health and Citizenship'. Her prize was the magnificent sum of £1. The seventeen-year-old Nellie ('Sister Ellen Mape') was fêted at a Rechabite meeting, with some of the movement's top officials present, despite being feisty enough openly to criticise the 'old fossils' who ran the organisation. She called her piece 'The

Rechabite Order in the New Century'. This is what she wrote,
first on the back of the red progress cards she used in her job at
the steelworks, before making a fair copy:

One hundred years ago, eleven men of Salford sat down
and – well, to cut a long story short – founded the
Rechabite Order. These eleven men were possessed of noble
ideals, and a host of new ideas. The ideals have remained
noble and always will do, but the ideas are no longer new.
We forget that as the order grows older so also do its
methods, and if we allow them to become dusty they are
likely to form the mud that chokes the stream of progress.

It is all very well to sit safe and secure on the lofty
heights of idealism and to say 'We are Rechabites. Our aim
is to promote thrift and temperance. Not for all the world
will we climb down.' Oh, yes, that may sound very well in
*The Arabian Nights* or somewhere like that, but we are
dealing with the world not the clouds, so we must use
worldly methods. And to carry the simile further, we must
guard against making our intentions cloudy. I am fully
aware of the fact that no member would deny that they
were a Rechabite, but does he go out of his way to let the
general public know all about it? I think not. You may ask
whose fault is that. I'll tell you. It is nobody's fault and it is
everybody's fault.

Let us survey the object of our attack – the Brewers. Yes,
give them a capital letter, not for importance sake, but to
keep it ever before our eyes. The Brewers are paying more
and more attention to youth, doing all in their power to
form new drinkers – and what are we doing to combat
this? We pay quite a lot of attention to the juveniles, and
even that could be improved upon, but that is not the most
serious problem. It is what we call the young people we
must cater for. There is only one rule – youth loves a gay
time.

The Brewers are building new public houses everywhere with the most modern architecture and conveniences. Every new estate has a new hotel. Do we see a corresponding number of Rechabite tents? No, we do not. The Brewers provide gaiety, music, dancing, concerts and a good time generally. If the public, the great legions outside the Order, will not adapt themselves to our way of thinking, we must adapt our Order to cater for them. I know that this sounds like rank heresy, but it is true.

The only way to win this struggle is to fight the enemy with its own weapons. This can be done if only the older people (if this were a speech, I should say 'old fossils') will take themselves off into the country and let a nice fresh breeze blow away all the deep-seated, antiquated ideas back to where they belong, with the samplers and anti-macassars. To all this bombardment you may reply that we do have social events – yes, I grant you that, but only for Rechabites. Don't tell me that we must focus our attention on the members we already have. We should not worry. If we employ ourselves to further the cause of Rechabitism outside the Order, we won't lose anyone. I will admit that a few people need stimulation to keep them even mildly active, but if we restrict our energies to within the bounds of the Order, where will it get us? Exactly nowhere.

Here in Manchester, we have done something about it. We have formed a Youth League of Service, which has a Concert Party. That is something along the [right] lines, but we have still far to go. I am very young and you may say very foolish, and I haven't travelled much. But judging from the places I do know, the Order is, to use an old Lancashire saying, very backward in coming forward. I will probably be put where all the young people belong, in my place, and told that the Order is not a film star, but I'll guarantee that if Miss La Glamorous or somebody's publicity agent were in the job, I should have a far different song to sing.

I have never had the opportunity of saying these things in public. I never realised until the Centenary Celebrations how little people really did know about the Rechabite Order. Now these ideas, opinions or whatever you like to call them are down on paper. I feel a conscious lightening, I can look forward with renewed hope to a new century and new ideas.

The 'old fossils' of the Rechabite movement did not take kindly to Nellie's comments. The *Rechabite Magazine* of August 1937 reports:

Manchester District No. 1. On 25 June, an interesting ceremony was carried out at the quarterly meeting of the 'Star of Bradford' Tent, No. 10. Sister Ellen Mape,[2] winner of the first prize in grade 1 of the essay competition, was the chief guest of the evening. The meeting was well attended, and also included Juvenile Tent Officers and TKE [temperance knowledge examination] Certificate winners, who were present by invitation of the Adult Tent. The DCR, Bro. T. Hughes (Secretary of the Tent), said that they were proud of the distinction which Sister Mape had brought to the Tent, and of the fact that she was using her ability as a Juvenile Superintendent. He also called upon Bro. S. Booth, D. Ex., to present the Certificate and award of £1. Bro. Booth remarked that this was one of the most pleasant duties he had carried out in the District. He knew that Sister Mape would be the first to admit that it was not she alone who won the distinction, but that credit must be given to the Superintendents who, during her time in the Juvenile Tent, had quietly and consistently instilled into her the great principles of Rechabitism.

Sister Mape, in a charming little speech, briefly responded. She read her essay to the assembled members (the subject: Alcohol, Health and Citizenship), and it was received with well-merited applause. TKE Certificates were presented to Sister W. Mape [Nellie's younger sister Winnie] and Sister E. Hughes, as well as to Sister Ellen Mape herself.

## The Independent Order of Rechabites

The Order began in Salford, England in 1835. These original Rechabites took their name from the Old Testament leader Rechab, who instructed his tribe to refrain from drinking alcohol. It is recorded that the tribe was tested and remained loyal to its principles. During the Industrial Revolution these ideals came to the fore once again and people joined together to help each other prevent the damage to families caused through the abuse of alcohol. Applicants for membership to the Order were required to sign a pledge of total abstinence in order to gain admission. Throughout the years, members of the Order relied upon it for assistance during times of sickness and death, and enjoyed the feeling of security knowing that in the face of misfortune help would be extended.

The IOR had its roots in earlier temperance organisations and sick and funeral societies such as the Salford Temperance Burial Society. One common problem was that part of the money set aside for funerals was often being spent on drink to celebrate the occasion. The *Preston Temperance Advocate* of July 1835 reported:

It is well known that, according to Act of Parliament, no part of the funds is allowed to be spent in Liquor. Notwithstanding, many of the [Burial] Societies evade this, and spend considerable sums in this way, to the great disadvantage of these institutions. The Burial Society now held at the Weaver's Arms compels every person who receives a funeral allowance to spend 4s in liquor.

No doubt the landlord of the pub where the burial club was based had an influence on how the money was spent!

By the 1930s the Rechabite Order had well over a million members, and there were branches in almost every town and sizeable village in the country. In 1935, the Star of Bradford Tent had 539 members and assets of more than £2,600. The Order was not just a temperance movement, but was also very much a welfare organisation at a time when the state provided only minimal protection for the old, sick and unemployed. However, the Rechabites did administer social welfare schemes which were approved and supported by the government.

The 1935 centenary celebrations were held at the Belle Vue Zoological Gardens, Manchester, a short bus ride from Gibbon Street where Nellie lived. Some 90,000 teetotallers assembled for music, demonstrations and pageantry. The pageant in the stadium was performed by over 3,000 members, mostly juveniles. There was an audience of more that 4,000 in the King's Hall to hear the movement's High Chief Ruler, Bro. Robert Anderson, JP of Darlington, open the proceedings. The main speaker was the Rt Hon. Walter Runciman MP, President of the Board of Trade. The vote of thanks was moved by Sir David Shackleton KCB.

The Blackburn District alone sent a party of 900 members on one of 130 special trains hired for the day. This particular special train was so long it overlapped some village station platforms at both ends, and in one case three stops had to be made at the same village. At one point, the engine driver could not see the guard, with the result that the guard was left behind. The driver had to decouple the engine and go back down the track to rescue his stranded colleague. All this caused the train to arrive back at Blackburn so late that many members missed their last trams and buses. The 2,500-strong Durham County contingent left Central Station, Newcastle, at 6.40 a.m. and arrived at Manchester at 12 noon.

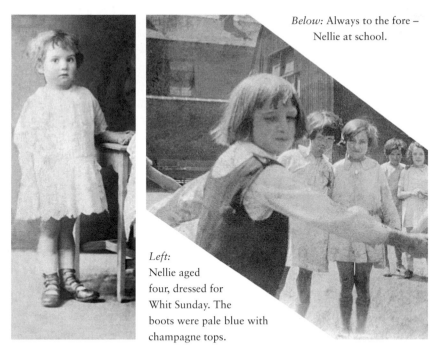

*Below:* Always to the fore –
Nellie at school.

*Left:*
Nellie aged
four, dressed for
Whit Sunday. The
boots were pale blue with
champagne tops.

Nellie's school class, 1932.

My Father
Front Row
2nd from Left

THE BOYS FROM FRANCE

'The Boys from France', during the First World War.
Nellie's father, Jack Mape, is in the front row, second
from the left.

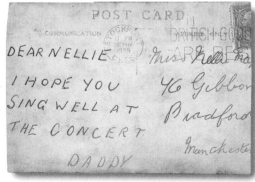

POST CARD

COMMUNICATION                    BRITISH GOODS

DEAR NELLIE      Miss Nellie Ma
I HOPE YOU       46 Gibbon
SING WELL AT     Bradford
THE CONCERT
                 Manchester
DADDY

Jack Mape's postcard to his six-year-old daughter
Nellie, from the convalescent home.

Nellie's mother, Ada Mape, née Cottrell, 1951.

*Above, left:* Young Stan with his mother, Eleanor. *Right:* Stan and his father, John.

*Below:* The 'Blue Hoodlums' Band – Stan is on the left.

Gibbon Street, 1963. Nellie's house (no. 76) is five doors along from the corner shop. (*By permission of Manchester Archives and Local Studies, Manchester City Council*)

Children playing in Philips Park.

The backs of Gibbon Street, 1963. (*By permission of Manchester Archives and Local Studies, Manchester City Council*)

The view from Gibbon Street along Sidney Street and across the canal to the power station cooling towers, 1963. (*By permission of Manchester Archives and Local Studies, Manchester City Council*)

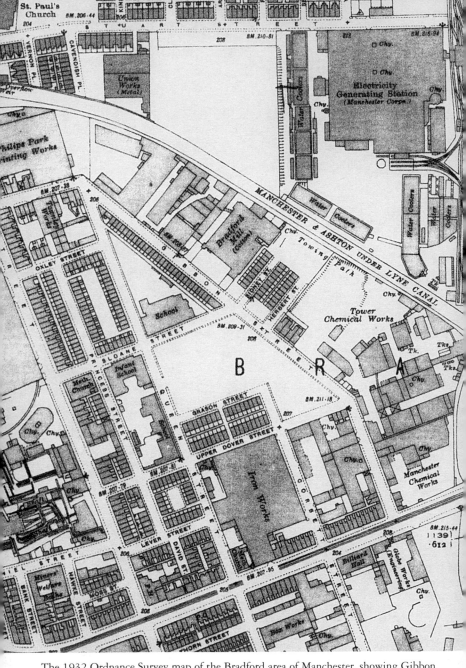

The 1932 Ordnance Survey map of the Bradford area of Manchester, showing Gibbon Street (centre), where Nellie grew up. (*Reproduced by permission of the Ordnance Survey © Crown copyright, 1932*)

Auntie Louie, Ada's sister.

Auntie Ginny (Jane), Ada's sister.

Marsland's cotton mill, where Nellie's mother, Ada, and her sister Louie worked. Gibbon Street runs across the front of the mill, the Manchester and Ashton-under-Lyme canal behind. The mill is seen here in 1987 after most of the houses surrounding it had been demolished. *(Reproduced by permission of English Heritage, National Monuments Record. © Crown copyright NMR)*

Kitty Gaskin next-door

*Above, left:* The Gaskin boys who lived next door at No. 78.

*Above, right:* Kitty Gaskin from No. 78.

*Left:* Agnes and Kate Read from No. 56.

*Above:* Nellie, aged seventeen, wins a national essay-writing competition. Her prize – £1. (*From* Juvenile Rechabite, *September 1937, by permission*)

*Right:* Nellie's temperance knowledge certificate.

INDEPENDENT ORDER of RECHABITES.

## Temperance Knowledge Examination.

Name of Successful Candidate :

Sister/~~Brother~~ *Nellie Make*

Tent No. *9* District No. *1*

Award gained *1st class*

in Division *4*

Have you previously gained a T.K.E. Certificate ? ...........

If so, do you desire another Certificate

or a Book ? ...........

**Note.**—Each successful candidate is entitled to receive a certificate showing the award gained. To those whose papers have been marked "Honours" 2/6 in cash is given in addition to a certificate. Candidates who have been successful in a previous T.K. examination may receive a book in lieu of another certificate if they so desire.

**FILL IN THIS FORM** and return it to the District Secretary as soon as possible.

*Right:* Young lovers, Stan and Nellie, in Castleton, Derbyshire, 1938.

*Left:* Stan's business card, *c.* 1938.

*Above:* Lt Stanley Wood RNVR, 1943.

*Below:* HMS *Royal Arthur* 1941/42. Stan is on the back row, far right.

*Above, left:* Glamour girl Nellie on a camping trip before the war.

*Above, right:* Bathing belle Nellie by the River Wye, 1939.

*Right:* Nellie 'in 14th heaven' with two chaps, Buxton, 1939.

*Above:* Nellie at war.

*Right:* Stan and Nellie on their wedding day, 11 July 1940. Nellie was four months pregnant.

*Opposite, top left:* Nellie and Chris, 1942.

*Far right:* Nellie in a fur cape, Dawlish, July 1944.

*Right:* Nellie and baby Penelope, 1945.

The Wood family. Left to right, back row: Stan, Nellie, John Wood (Stan's father). Front: Mary Brigham (Stan's gran), Chris, Eleanor Wood (Stan's mother).

Nellie and Chris, 1945.

*Opposite, top:* Nellie and friends in their posh frocks.

*Opposite, bottom:* An A' level Geography Field Trip, 1966. Nellie is at the back on the right.

Helen Wood MA, 1978.

Nellie and Stan still together, 1990.

All of Belle Vue's liquor bars were closed for the occasion, and all advertisements for alcoholic drink were either removed or covered up. To refresh the crowd (and it was a very hot day) there were vast quantities of mineral water and ice cream. An astonishing 120,000 bottles of lemonade and 60,000 bottles of milk were drunk. Water taps were fitted throughout the grounds. The police presence, scarcely necessary on such a sober if joyous occasion, amounted to one superintendent, three inspectors and forty constables. Numerous children were lost, but all were restored to their parents before the end of the proceedings.[3]

The Independent Order of Rechabites operates in a very different environment today. While its services have been greatly extended, the basic principles of mutuality and self-help, on which IOR was founded, are just as evident. Today the Order operates as a friendly society, offering services in the areas of investments, health benefits funds, funeral benefits and social activities through the fraternal membership, temperance education and scholarships.

There has been one further significant change for the Rechabites in this century. In the year 2000, the Order gained its first-ever woman leader in electing Margaret McDonald as Lady Chairman (the term 'High Chief Ruler' is now no longer used). Nellie, in her own words 'a lifelong abstainer', and very much an advocate for the total equality of women and men, was still alive. I wonder if she knew. She would certainly have approved. After all, at the age of seventeen she had the temerity to tell the 'old fossils' of the Rechabites that they had to get modern!

Nora Mape was also an active member of the Rechabites, along with her younger sisters Nellie and Winnie. Aged just twelve years, Nora was awarded a magnificent framed certificate (a huge thing) as Companion of the Legion of Honour for 1929, and also of the Hope of Bradford Tent, Manchester District No. 1, Salford Unity. I found it among Nellie's possessions. Mind, she threw nothing away!

Years later, Nellie wrote to the Rechabites:

28th June 1992
Independent Order of Rechabites

Dear Sir
First my 'credentials'. I am an old abstainer. Joined Hope of
Bradford Tent in the early twenties, loved every minute of it,
entered the TKE (successful) and was part of the Rechabite
Queen and Court (Manchester, of course) and the Centenary
Pageant in Queen's Park.

I came to see later that these years had been invaluable to
me, in the true educational sense, contributing the development which later took me through 'O' and 'A' levels, university and a teaching career. It is only recently, now seventy-two,
that I have begun to write.[4] I completed an article on my own
young days from a specialized angle, how poor families
managed for clothes in the Depression, and I would now like
to go further into my childhood experiences, encouraged by
the reception of my first effort.

Yours sincerely
Helen Wood

## Politics

From an early age, politics was never far from Nellie's mind,
even when she was enjoying herself. Nellie recalled that when
she went camping in Heaton Park with the White Heather Fund
before the war, they sang a parody of 'There is a Happy Land',
with its references to the 'children of the workers'. Nellie wrote:

When Election Day came round, we would shout 'Who y'r
voting for?' to other children outside the polling booth.
Other children whispered that Ida's father was a com-

munist. On enquiring of my friend what communists actually did, I was told that they 'keep marching to London'. On voting days, I remember paper balls on the end of a long string, whirled around threateningly and used on occasion. There was a popular election ditty, directed at Flanagan, the Conservative candidate:

> Flanagan fell in a box of eggs, parleyvoo
> Flanagan fell in a box of eggs, parleyvoo
> Flanagan fell in a box of eggs
> And all the yeller ran down his legs
> Inky pinky parleyvoo.

Nellie wrote out the song she used to sing in her Young Communist days:

> Fly higher and higher and higher
> Our emblem the Soviet Star
> And every propeller is roaring (Red Front!)
> Defending the USSR
> But for the wage slaves
> And the toiling masses
> A song of hope in our propellers whirr
> We drop them leaflets while we bomb their bosses
> The first Red Air Force of the world.

Stan's diary records:

3 MARCH 1948
Wife has been in touch with Russia. 'Don't use the phrase "left-winger" – it's so out-of-date.'

1 OCTOBER 1963
She [Nellie] has just remembered that when she was expecting Penelope [born 1945] she was studying a Chekhov Play – *Uncle Vanya* – very interesting, for a part in a play being produced by Soviet Friendship Group.

# 8

# *Managing*

As she grew up and looked at the world around her, Nellie was very conscious of social differences. She knew her family and her neighbours were poor. She herself often went hungry, but she never resented her circumstances. In her teens, Nellie put her energies into social and political action through the Rechabites and the Young Communists. As an adult, Nellie became upwardly mobile, determined to raise the standard of living of her family. In this she succeeded magnificently, making sure all her four children got a good education, something denied to her as a child. All four of her children went to university, as did Nellie herself in later life.

In accepting her family's low position in society when she was growing up, Nellie was never resigned to her fate. It was simply that she and everyone around her made the best of what they had available. There was a huge amount of self-help and community support. Any spare food or surplus clothing and footwear was immediately made available to relatives, friends and neighbours. This mutual help was offered and accepted without shame or obligation on either side. It was just the done thing. The poor helped the poor to make life a little more bearable for everybody.

In the absence of all but the most basic support from the state, the people of Gibbon Street and thousands of other similar streets did not sit back and wait for help to arrive. They did everything they could to help themselves. The people of Gibbon Street prided themselves on their respectability. They were not lawless or rebellious. Crime was relatively absent, the most common misdemeanour being drunk and disorderly behaviour. Gibbon (Empire) Streeters were conscious that there were other people worse off than they were, who lived in a more disreputable part of town. This is how Nellie saw it:

No matter how bad things were in the twenties and thirties, the hard-pressed residents of the industrial North never lost their pride. They knew they were poor, but they always kept their self-respect. And our terraced streets were not slums! Whatever the varying views of the Empire Streeters on things in general, on one subject there could be only one opinion. We did not live in a slum. There were slums in other parts of Manchester, Angel Meadow in particular, though few Empire Street residents had ever been there. Slums were dirty, full of ragged, neglected children, and dangerous to walk round after dark. The 'never fewer than two bobby [police] patrol' theory was universally believed.

Each house had its own backyard with flush lavatory. Not like the slums, which those of us with relatives in Salford knew about, which had communal yards and facilities to match. Rents in Empire Street were seven shillings a week. There were no gardens, and just one cold-water tap. Houses with hot and cold water were a distant dream of paradise; likewise bathrooms and indoor sanitation.

Missing the rent to buy, say, shoes was considered quite OK. The rent man would call on Monday morning (washing day), hammering on the door. People hid under the stairs. He was known to have spies who reported who was really in. Our landlord collected his own rents. He was always most polite, greeting the woman of the house with 'My good woman' or 'My dear madam'. However, he was never known to do any repairs or painting.

We knew we were poor, of course, but the problem of finding the wherewithal for these things was never paraded in front of us. We had implicit faith that what could be done, would be done. I had no idea of my own family's domestic budget – it was not considered appropriate for children to know. I realise now, that at times the only possible solution must been a clothing check, and the long drag of weekly payments, not much different from the dreaded tallyman of Victorian times.

Most families were large, several in double figures. Unlike the dwellers in country villages, Empire Streeters were not able to relieve overcrowding in their two-bedroomed houses by sending the older girls out to service. Such a move would have been despised, quite apart from the fact that any older girls who couldn't get a job in mill, factory or machine room at fourteen would scarcely have been suitable material for the middle-class world of cap and apron.

There were many domestic rows about the sixpences and shillings that went to the bookie. Small loans could be obtained from money clubs and 'diddlum' clubs. One way of raising short-term credit was to do a bundle of washing for a neighbour without charge. It would be washed and ironed, and then taken straight to the pawnshop until Friday. It was the same again the following Monday. Even on the poverty line, as many Empire Streeters were, a certain basic etiquette was observed. In this way, various little shifts and shortages, inescapable in those Depression years, were kept within the family circle.

Of course, within our own circle of acquaintances, we had the entrée to each other's houses, but only within reason. Empire Street bore no resemblance to *Coronation Street* in the easy popping in and out and friendly helpfulness supposedly inherent in the Northern way of life. However, it was possible to walk in without knocking, as most front doors opened with a turn of a knob. In fact, a knock at the door usually signified the rent man, or the doctor's man (collecting sixpenny instalments off the bill), or some other equally unwelcome visitor.

Good manners required that a visiting neighbour should step just inside the door and call out 'Are you there?', even if the lady of the house was visible. Subsequent social behaviour depended on the purpose of the call, the reputation of the caller, and the attitude of the housewife to neighbouring as a way of life. It was disapproved of in my family. Being better off in Empire Street meant having no more than two children, with father working; or else a large family with the older ones in jobs and tipping up most of their wages to their Mam.

Stories of paying for entrance to the cinema or theatre with jam-jars still surface from time to time. It seems highly unlikely that cinemas ever needed to bother with these, even if it had been desirable. Every Saturday they could always count on a queue of pushing, shoving kids with pennies in their hands. It may have happened, and probably did, that some of those pennies had been raised by returning jam-jars, worth, I think, a halfpenny each. Many families, like my own, never saw a full pot of jam, but sent a child to the corner shop with a saucer for small amounts from a giant jar. This is one of the more believable snippets of oral history, but like the jam-jar entrance fees, and the pregnant mill-workers slogging away until the very last moment, these figure in so many reminiscences that one has less than perfect faith in every example.

In his book *Leisure, Gender and Culture in Salford & Manchester 1900–1939*, Andrew Davies questions the assumptions about working-class life in this period as lacking evidence. His opinions derive from oral interviews and more recent writings. I was surprised to discover, on returning to education in my forties, that the South of England and other areas did not suffer from the slump as the North did. Davies refers to the vivid images of fish-and-chip eating and holidays at Blackpool for workers of this period. He says that leisure activities give insights into social life, living standards and relations within families. He gives walking in the park as one example of free leisure. Davies mentions women going to the cinema, taking children if they had to. My children went to the cinema by themselves as soon as they were able.

The words 'poor' and 'poverty' were seldom heard in Empire Street. In fact, poverty was almost a forbidden word. Crying poverty was a socially unacceptable manoeuvre in most homes. People who indulged in it were heartily despised. You might be 'a bit pushed for money just now'. An Auntie who was relating how the 'dog lawrence' officer had climbed her backyard wall to discover if she had a dog for which she had not paid the licence (she had), put it this way: 'Half-crowns were not too plentiful at that particular moment.'

We often saw one particular ragman at church on a Sunday, dressed appropriately for the day, instead of in his weekday garb. This transformation was often commented on by people who had noticed, and they thoroughly approved of it. A ragman should dress like a ragman when pushing his cart on a weekday. Joe was considered to be a cut above the others, and entitled to his Sunday suit. The corporation muck cart, with its high sloping sides with sacks and tin baths hanging on the back, was surprisingly very clean. The driver was a lovely man, but it caused some surprise in the street that one couple were friendly with the muckman and went out for a drink with him at the weekend.

Kids generally did all right. If you were lucky, you got three halfpence a week pocket money, a penny for the pictures and a halfpenny for toffees – 'sweets' was reckoned to be a soppy word. Pennies could be earned going on errands, picking a bucket of cinders, fetching a quarter of coal (price 6*d*) – bring your own truck.

Stan's diary records:

4 APRIL 1962

Financial structure. [The Mape family] were on public assistance (PA) as the father was not able-bodied. It didn't make any difference what kids earned. Soul-destroying (means test). Only way they could get clothes was to go and live elsewhere [i.e. move house]. 'Facing a Board' meant terrible questioning about your means. The idea was to get as many families off PA as possible. Mother [Ada] must have been a very good manager. Worst-off poor families had to borrow something by Thursday, 2/6 [half a crown] or so, from people who were working. Moral obligation to lend. Mother didn't work after Bernard [her youngest child] was born. Lots of wives used to have all their clothes off rag-and-bone carts. Never had anything new. To come to school in a new frock – amazement! Gingham. The locals considered themselves quite well off – father never beat them. No child beaters in Gibbon Street. Nor did anyone go to jail.

Wife [Nellie] remembers when police gave free clogs to children. You went in a large basement at Mill Street and there were hundreds and hundreds of pairs of clogs. Priest once bought her a pair out of his own money – very good clogs with a clasp. And you could make lovely sparks (I never knew the joy of making sparks – never had a pair of clogs).

## Managing for Clothes

Nellie was a lifelong member of the Costume Society and was their publications secretary for twenty years. She wrote for the society's journal, encouraged by the editor, Dr Ann Saunders. The following article was published in the *Journal of the Costume Society* in 1993. Its full title was 'Managing for Clothes in the Depression Years of the 20s and 30s; or, Keeping Up with the Social Calendar in Empire Street'. It was based on the chapter Nellie had written for 'Empire Street', entitled 'Clothes'. It was my privilege and pleasure to read extracts from this chapter at my mother's (non-religious) funeral in 2001.

Monica Dickens recalls, in the semi-autobiographical novel of her wartime factory experiences, *The Fancy*, how her relationships with her fellow workers miraculously improved once she learned how to respond appropriately to the friendly query, 'How are you managing?' To be able to 'manage' and discuss with others methods of countering the bleakness and discomforts of wartime Britain had an importance in human terms far beyond any immediate practical benefits.

The mothers of families in the late twenties and early thirties had an even harder task than the wartime mothers in keeping clothes on the backs and shoes on the feet of their children. Shortage of clothing was nothing compared to the scarcity of jobs during the Slump, and the consequent acute shortage of money. Nevertheless, most families managed, and managed very well. This article describes, from personal experience, how it was done in one small district of industrial Manchester – how almost every family endeavoured to keep up with the demands of the social calendar as they knew it, and how they protected their children, as far as possible, from the humiliation of being excluded from school activities which depended on cash expenditure for special clothing.

Leaving aside for the moment purely seasonal demands, the burden of merely sending several children to school fit to be seen, every day of the school year, was onerous enough. Winter was more difficult than summer, naturally. To provide weatherproof shoes and warm outer clothing was a continuing problem, and one not easily solved. Most mothers and unmarried aunties were skilled in converting old topskirts into kilts for little girls, and steaming the crinkles out of the unravelled wool from old jumpers, before crocheting it into warm scarves, 'tommyshanters' and hug-me-tights. Anything to keep out the cold.

Summer must have been a great relief, if only because the 'clean pinny' philosophy could then be brought into play. Most mothers called a cotton frock a pinny, much to our disgust, and they seemed to feel that the donning of a nicely ironed cotton garment, of whatever age or provenance, conferred something of the aura of virtuous respectability inherent in the long white school pinafores of their own early days.

A cotton frock was easily run up out of nearly anything you could mention, and the huge rack of clean garments hanging from most working-class ceilings was proof enough of the widespread belief in the 'clean pinny' school of thought, and clear evidence of the hard work and contrivance of the principal believers.

Our little world, Empire Street, consisted of one long row of about forty small terraced houses, and two short side streets running off it. There were also seven assorted factories, but although the homegoing workers were often good for a cake or an apple, and one lot in particular for endless eatables and bottles of pop at Christmas, any reference to clothing needs from one side or the other would have been reckoned distinctly out of order. Local families tended to be large, quite a few in double figures, but as far as babies were concerned, there was no problem in dressing them, at least for the initial non-active three months in long clothes. I expect the middle-class mothers who would be the original sources of the pretty 'needlework' (broderie Anglaise) gowns, the barras and binders and the rest of the traditional paraphernalia then considered essential, passed them on in good condition, probably via one of the useful wardrobe ladies who visited the more prosperous southern suburbs for that purpose. In Empire Street, common prudence suggested that such items would be needed again before too long, but the local mothers assumed that the ladies of Cheadle and Didsbury either had money to burn, or knew something, at present unknown, to 'the rest of us'. At three months the baby was supposed to be 'shortened', but this was something of a moveable feast and could be put off in very cold weather, or for any other reason, true or false, if one was not quite ready. Older people still spoke of little boys being 'britched' at about three years of age, and tried to convince the local children that boys even older used to wear frocks like little girls. This was considered to be an old wives' tale. I never believed this at the time, knowing no better, and certainly never saw any examples myself.

Even in our poor neighbourhood you wouldn't see a schoolchild in rags or the ubiquitous 'single garment' of the Victorian street tales. No one at my school would have dared! Our headmistress was a great one for calling the whole school together and giving us firm opinions on all kinds of desirable and undesirable behaviour. Included in these marathon lectures was plenty of advice on how to dress. She particularly detested very short skirts, referring to them as 'little better than a bodice with a frill on'. Another teacher, usually somewhat severe, but in this instance trying to be helpful, when stressing the importance of clean underwear for personal pride and a healthy body, went on to advise us, if we had only a limited wardrobe, to wash out one item each day and dry it overnight. Some of us could only contemplate with horror the reaction of our mothers to this reckless dab-washing and expenditure of hot water and soap. We often speculated on such occasions on the kind of world these teachers must live in.

On one occasion, the reason for which escapes my memory, the better-off girls in my class of ten-year-olds

were asked to bring in surplus garments for distribution to
the rest of it. The haul was unexpectedly large, and the
rumour went that our class teacher, Miss H., had
abstracted the best of these for some alleged nieces of her
own, and much indignation raged round the class in
consequence. Donors of identifiable garments held inquests
in the playground, but no reliable conclusion was ever
decided upon. Possibly some of the recipients did not care
to admit that they had taken part in this unusual charity
handout. Certainly, the pale blue coat with the little square
buttons, so often enquired after by the giver, was never
discovered hanging on the Standard Four coatpegs. More
probably, some behind-the-scenes official conclave had
decided that any good quality items would only find their
way straight to the pawnshop and had prudently indulged
in some preliminary sifting.

The pawnshop itself, besides its primary purpose, was
quite a good source of second-hand clothing from
unredeemed pledges. These were often a better buy than
similar items from the second-hand shops because of their
long periods resting unworn on the pawnshop shelves.
There wasn't a lot of choice; you stated your requirements
and one or two likely garments were rapidly produced
from the mysterious back premises. Size and price being
usually acceptable, the deal was then struck. Naturally, you
didn't let the neighbours know.

Another good source of clothing bargains, as long as you
had a little cash in your pocket, was the band of long-
established and vastly experienced market-stall auctioneers,
usually called Old Maggie or Sarah Anne, one or two of
whom were brilliant stand-up comediennes in their own
right. Week after week they stood long hours behind their
mountainous heaps of assorted garments, snatching up
each one in turn and displaying its charms with swift
balletic movements, accompanied by a running commen-

tary which assured them an interested audience for most of the day. This is where you went if you wanted something special, a dance frock or a winter coat at the lowest possible price. It was a thrilling exercise in purchasing skill to guess when the asking price would go no lower, and then to jump in and secure the prize.

As a last resort, there was always the ragman, with his handcart of assorted cast-offs, but nobody cared to admit to wearing anything off the ragman's cart. This was one step lower than buying from the pawnshop, and there was always that 'You don't know where it's been' feeling about such purchases.

Household articles were different. We once acquired from this source a large trunk to use as a bedding box, which proved to be full of wide-skirted and flounced cotton dresses, which were rapidly unpicked to provide many clean pinnies, mostly of the ubiquitous lilac hue, known to us as 'morve' and to our mothers as 'eelitroop'. Some mothers thought too much fuss was made about what colour things were. Any complaints about the everlasting 'beege' costumes of the twenties' cast-offs which came our way were dismissed with the scornful accusation that we hankered after 'sky-blue pink with a finny-haddock border', the traditional comment on the taste of a person given to wearing vulgar multicoloured outfits.

Free clothes could usually be had by families who knew the right charities to approach, and had a good tale to tell. Some people shamelessly milked these sources, but in my family 'crying poverty' was very much despised. Not that a helping hand from time to time was totally ruled out, but it should never be begged for or even hinted at.

For example, when the good ladies of the parish sent a supply of hand-knitted vests like medieval body armour for distribution round the school, if a couple came to you, you took them home like everyone else. Likewise the ticket for free clogs from the Police Charity, a good supply of which came every year. This was a girls' school, and girls in general did not like clogs, any more than they welcomed the high-leg boots which some old-fashioned mothers still insisted on in the winter. Boys were different: they enjoyed striking sparks on the pavement and other undesirable activities, where the heavier and tougher the footwear, the more satisfying the effect.

The free clogs were fitted on in a large hall in the centre of Manchester, straps for the girls, clasps or lace-ups for the boys. They needed endless softening, but, in spite of this, painful blisters were almost inevitable. Perhaps, like the ticklish vests, there was an element of penance in these charitable offerings.

The tradition of new clothes for Whitsuntide was, and is, very strong in Lancashire as in a number of other places. It was universally observed in Empire Street, no matter what the rough drunken inhabitants of such slums as we had only vaguely heard about, where the policemen only ventured in twos, might choose to do. Of course, the new clothes were seldom literally new – that was taken for granted – but they gave us as much pleasure as if we had been offered the pick of all that Kendal Milnes [a department store] could provide.

It depended on the composition of the family which fresh items were needed in order to make a decent show. If there were several girls in reasonable sequence, the essential white frocks stayed safely in the pawnshop from one Whit to another, rather in the style of rich ladies putting their furs in cold storage for the summer. They could always be got out for a first communion or confirmation. The usual style of Magyar bodice and flounced skirt [traditional mid-European costume] lent itself admirably to taking in and letting out, and, together with judicious passing on as the girls grew, the dresses could be made to do for years. My own family experience followed this pattern. Our two needlework, three-tiered, white best frocks were pieced out and passed on as long as possible, until they had to be replaced by two home-made matt satin masterpieces; no flounces, but trimmed with swansdown. Each subsequent year saw the trimming unpicked, carefully washed, then slowly waved in front of the fire to fluff it up, before being reattached.

The white dresses and the rest of the customary seasonal costume meant more than just keeping up with the Joneses. It went right to the roots of personal pride and self-respect, and a determination not to be crushed by hard times and adverse circumstances. The ambitions of the very poorest never soared beyond the white dresses and cheap white-canvas pumps, but where a little money was coming in, perhaps with a couple of grown-up lads in work, the second-hand underground railroad, which passed bundles of once-fashionable garments from safe house to safe house, provided a 'try before you buy' selection service which in the circumstances was second to none.

The secrecy was necessary because many of the customers, and the small-time intermediaries, were on benefit of some kind, and more than one poor woman was called before the authorities in those means-test years to answer the accusation that she was running a business. These sound, good-quality costumes and underwear were garnered from better-off homes by the professional ward-robe dealers, and filtered down to Empire Street level through the usual retail channels. Of course, we never got the pick of the crop, but I can dimly remember a fur hood and cape when I was about five years old, courtesy of a generous auntie, I think.

The fruit of all the planning and contrivance began to emerge soon after breakfast on Whit Sunday morning, when groups of well-scrubbed children, dressed to the nines by Empire Street standards, would be seen about the streets, getting in as many inspection visits as possible and raking in the welcome pennies which tradition would have scarcely denied them on this occasion, the highlight of the year for many. Mostly these pennies rapidly found their way to the sweetshop or ice-cream cart, but one occasionally heard shocked whispers of families where their mother took the money off them as soon as the children got home. I learned, as I got older, that the donors were perfectly aware that the children would have to tip up their legitimate gains at home, but would still not deprive the young ones of the pride and pleasure of temporary wealth.

I have often wondered if the group of barge children in very old-fashioned long print dresses, seen in our neighbour-hood one Sunday morning long ago, were on a similar ex-pedition. We were appallingly rude to them, ridiculing their strange accents, and adopting their desperate response, 'What are ya larfing at? Is it us cloase?', as an unfailing trigger for hysterical laughter for weeks afterwards. For those of us who would be walking in the religious processions which are such a glorious and important part of Manchester's heritage, the Sunday morning's rather formal round of calls was merely the overture to the greater doings later in the week. Local parish walks took place on Sunday afternoon.

We partakers of the pomp and circumstance of either of the two big days, Whit Monday or Whit Friday, tended to view these lesser shows rather patronizingly, but no doubt the expense, the preparations and the anxiety that all should go well were felt as acutely, whatever the size of the proces-sion. As regards the two main events, the Protestants on Whit Monday and the Catholics on Whit Friday, no efforts were spared, physical, mental and financial, to maintain the magnificent reputation of these glorious spectacles, which brought the business and commercial centre of Manchester to a halt on these two official holidays, and according to many people 'for the best part of a week'.

There is no doubt that anyone privileged enough to watch these huge processions, colourful expressions of religious faith and traditional loyalty, as they threaded the traffic-free streets, converged on the city centre and assembled in Albert Square, would fully appreciate the visual beauty, the music, the flowers, the whole glorious pageant which lit up the heart of the city in those drab years. Along with that went immense pride that our city, our schools and churches, and ultimately the city's own children could put on such a show. The beautifully costumed little May and Rose Queens, the train-bearers, the cushion-bearers, every one a star to the family at home, represented tremendous sacrifices, willingly made to give each child that supreme moment of glory.

In recollection it is difficult to switch the mind's eye to the lines of boys, immaculate in new blazers and caps and well-polished shoes; they were there, but one remembers the girls above all. These, the chorus backing up the solo players, were perfection in the aforementioned white dresses, having their canvas shoes lovingly blancoed[1] and dried on a hundred windowsills that morning, with a new hanky and a few coppers to buy tea and a bun at Joe Lyons in the square,[2] were the end products of months of penny-pinching to pay for the floral regalia of the year: wreaths, baskets, posies or shepherd's crooks.

The final result on walking day was worth it all. We children, marching as we had been trained to do by the indefatigable Miss O behind our magnificent trio of priests – all tall men, a familiar Whit Friday spectacle in their tall black shiners – savoured every moment of our three bands, the cheering crowds who lined the route, and the sheer pride of being part of it all.

The May Queen just referred to would be a little girl of about seven years old, who had earlier played a major part in the annual May crowning in church. We followed this tradition in our own street enactment of a May ceremony, which owed very little to the maidens on the village green dancing round the maypole, nothing at all to John Ruskin (as far as I ever heard), had no religious element, and was entirely child-run and child-financed. For once, the hard-pressed mothers need never lift a finger.

Every street more or less had its own May Queen, the standards of costuming and performance showing wide variations, to say the least. Our three streets might have been an isolated village, judging by the rigid boundary lines indicating the area within which it was permissible for the mini 'court' to call and perform its little ceremony.

In strict chronological order, the street May Queens preceded Whitsuntide, but the Queen, her lace-curtain train and train-bearers, the cushion-bearer and often a herald as well, seems to me now to have been so closely a crib of the style of the great annual religious processions that it seems logical to position it here. Only in the later years did one fully appreciate the educational value of these events. The May Queen was only one of a number of street occasions which forced one to acquire what are now called 'life skills', elementary tactics to cope with whatever comes up.

In the two or three years during which the organisation of the Empire Street May Queen fell to my lot, I debated my choice of leading players, designed and made the tissue-paper costumes, turning the cuttings into aptly named artificial flowers for the garland, and rehearsed the rigmarole of sung snippets customarily used down our way. As I have mentioned, I foresaw no benefits further ahead than the party in our backyard (with white *and* brown bread), provisioned from the tin full of pennies we usually collected.

But I was wrong. Of the landmarks which punctuated the social calendar of Empire Street, some of them, like the annual pilgrimage to the fair at Daisy Nook on Good

Friday, with hard-boiled eggs and salmon-paste sandwiches, did not give rise to any particular wardrobe anxieties, and thus have no relevance here. But of the engagements involving dress matters, the annual school concert could prove the most nerve-racking and expensive.

All preliminary planning and decision-making was in the hands of the teachers; neither mothers nor children were involved at this stage. But it was laid down inescapably that if you could not pay for your costume, you couldn't be in it, and that was that. Few people would deprive their children of the pleasure of participation, and themselves of the family pride and local kudos if their child performed well, so they squeezed the threepences and sixpences out of the weekly budget somehow.

Half a crown was the average cost of the materials. The parish ladies and good reliable mothers with sewing machines made up the costumes dreamed up and cut out by the teachers. The outfits were new every year, and you could take yours home afterwards – for this was no corny, hastily thrown-together effort, but a colourful, enjoyable show, given for three nights, for which tickets were always in demand. So the teachers went off to the big warehouses in the city centre to choose the materials. We girls picked up what scraps of information we could by eavesdropping, because not one of the teachers divulged the secrets of what we would be wearing before they were forced to do so.

We tried to guess what the bundles of sewing sent to the selected mothers were intended for, and, as we older girls were conscripted for 'press-stud and tape' duty, we gradually put together a fair idea of what was going on, without this detracting one iota from our overwhelming surprise at the beauty of the finished products seen en masse on the night. Who would have thought our teachers could do it?

# 9

# *Our Street*

Nellie started writing her memoir in 1951, first naming it 'Empire Street' and then 'Our Street', and returning to it at intervals. In later years, Nellie showed terrific powers of memory in recalling her neighbours. What she remembered tallies closely with the records of the period. Jack and Ada Mape, Ada listed on the register as a weaver, lived at No. 76 Gibbon Street. The corner shop at the end of the row, Nos 86–90, was run by the Barnshaw family.

Our knowledge of our neighbours and their houses varied. We knew every person in our row by sight. Some we knew fairly well, and there were a few families of whom we saw quite a lot. Since my mother never 'neighboured', this rather cut down adult contacts. Mother tended to ask uninvited visitors, 'Do you want anything?'

The Reads at No. 56 were a family of eight girls. Their mother Isabella was illiterate, so her husband Thomas read *Red Letter* and *Peg's Paper* to her, right through. I remember the Reads watering the pot (of tea) for the children when the parents had finished. The Reads' house had flag floors, but also an elaborate fender and fire irons. They were a happy family. Mrs Read liked to call in on her neighbours for a chat about nothing, which was most annoying to the more energetic housewives like my mother. Mrs Read took in washing for the loan of the bundle until the weekend. After washing and ironing, the bundle would be taken to the pawnshop for later recovery. Mr Read was well in with the Legion. He could 'tell a good tale'.

The Mosses (No. 58, Frederick, Minnie, John) had a dog called Bongo who liked to visit other houses and was always welcome. Old Mrs Wood (Louisa Wood, No. 64) was an itinerant street singer. Her favourite song was 'Where Is My Wandering Boy Tonight?' Her daughter [who was always given a 'wole (sic) egg'] was no favourite of my mother, who thought she gave herself airs. Old Mrs Smith was almost a granny to us children.[1] She had two un-married sons who had been in France during the war. She had large framed photographs of them on the wall.

Mrs Diamond (Mary Anne Diamond at No. 66) was a very large lady. My father joked that the mill gates oppo-site had to be opened when she cleaned the front doorstep. She had two boys and an older girl. Mrs Diamond was said to have been a sweetheart of Stan Laurel in her younger [and presumably thinner] days. Mr Diamond (Walter) was very strict. He laid it on with the belt when his sons mis-behaved. Both boys had been away from home in what was called 'a reform school'. The neighbours blamed the con-stant leatherings in their childhood for the boys' behaviour.

Mr Diamond had been a champion clog dancer in his youth [as indeed had Stan Laurel]. My father, something of a joker, liked to lead him on to talk about his achievements in clog-dancing competitions. This would invariably end up with an offer to fetch his 'halbium' [album]. Mr Diamond would then proudly display his manly form in black tights, with his medals and his magnificent clogs.

The Talbots (Samuel and Esther, No. 72) were an elderly couple with no children. Their house seemed to us to be an abode of immense luxury, with its carpets, thick curtains and even a piano. They were kind to the local children, but otherwise kept very much to themselves. The Talbots were a good source of pennies for running errands.

The Balls (George and Emily) lived next door to us (No. 74). Mr Ball had a steady job. He was reputed to earn only £2 a week, but his position was secure. The Balls had a week's holiday at Blackpool every year. This was very unusual for our street, and a source of amazement to the neighbours. Otherwise, little was known of their business, but I was very friendly with their daughter Ivy, who joined in my favourite pretend games. On the other side was Mr Gaskins [George Gaskins at No. 78 – a widower?] who worked at the wireworks. He got mustard on his lunchtime sandwiches. He had two grown-up lads, both working (one was a particular favourite of mine), and two grown-up daughters. The elder daughter worked in the mill, the younger one, Kitty, at the asbestos works. The Gaskins's home was comfortably furnished. They had a sideboard with two prism ornaments under glass domes and wonderful wax fruit in the centre. The youngest boy, Arthur, was my age. He devotedly pushed me around in an old box, which was constantly breaking down and having its imaginary wheels repaired.

There were two houses where I particularly liked to go, and where I was usually welcome. One belonged to a married cousin who was very smart and up to date, and kept a store of comics and magazines under the cushion of her armchair. I say usually welcome, because having asked permission to look at a magazine I tended to read story after story and soon wore out that welcome!

There was another jolly family on the other side without a single cup, let alone a saucer. They managed with pot jam-jars and the odd broken vase when the supply of jars ran out. Their door was always wide open, and to see all these big lads round the table, supping away, both hands round a steaming jam-jar never failed to bring a smile or a sniff, according to taste, from passers-by. Many a subsequent social gathering was enlivened by the deadpan question, 'Has anybody got a broken vase?' Children kept the joke going for months. There must still be some ex-

Empire Streeters who are unable to hear of a mishap to some favourite flower container without an echo of a more simple and hilarious past.

The Saturday markets after dark, with their flaring naphtha lamps, attracted many people. One favourite was the toffee man, who made the toffee before your eyes, cooled it on a slab, stretched and twisted it into rainbow shapes, then snipped it into magnificent multicoloured humbugs, so big you could hardly get them into your mouth.

The 'corner lads' were aged sixteen to twenty-one. They were just a gang of youths, with no apparent use for girls. They organised and took charge of the giant bonfire on Bonfire Night, and made a good job of it. These lads were generally well regarded. People would send for a couple of corner lads to shift a wardrobe, for example, or to bring something on a handcart. Presumably, the householder saw them right. Their leisure activities included pavement card schools, tossing coins, shove-halfpenny, etc.

One of their main jobs was to collect and sell the still-burnable cinders from the croft. This patch of waste ground was not at that time divided from the canal by a wall, which was built later, when I was in my early teens. This part of the croft presumably belonged to the mill, as they used it as a tip for their spent fuel. I say spent, but these things are comparative. If you watched out for the giant barrows full of red-hot clinkers being wheeled up from the boiler room, you could get a bucket of burnable cinders easily with the aid of a home-made rake and a small shovel. No one ever used a sifter [sieve]. 'Is the tip coming out?' was the cry.

Cinders were free from the tip at the back of the mill. You had to get your own, or ask a corner lad to bring you a bucketful for a penny. Penny and halfpenny economy was current in Empire Street. A little hand-rake contrived out of an old shovel was invaluable, because all the best cinders arrived red hot in the huge barrows wheeled up the slope from the basement boiler room. The rake dealt with the giant clinkers, exposing a wealth of burnable fuel.

This free fuel helped to eke out the expensive coal from the coalman or coal yard, and the less expensive, but still barely affordable, bags of coke from the gasworks. The corner lads could get 2*d* for a bucket of good cinders, and they naturally saw to it that their superior rights in these matters were not encroached on. Fortunately, the corner lads never got up early, so before school was a good time to go, if you had a firm order from a hard-up neighbour. However, girls got only 1*d* a bucket.

'See if you can find a big lad to go to the coal yard,' was a common request from a neighbour. A quarter of coal cost 6*d*, I think. Heavy jobs, such as moving furniture, required the services of a corner lad. The big lad needed to have a cart available, usually a soapbox cart sporting cast-iron wheels from old mangles. The coal yard had a couple of small carts, but presumably they charged for these, the management was reluctant to lend them out. They may well have been doubtful of their safe return. The coal was weighed in a huge scoop-shaped scale.

I never went for more than a quarter hundredweight [28lb] of coal myself. That cost 6*d*, but many a time I obliged some harried housewife by finding her a big lad with a cart to fetch a half hundredweight [56lb]. In any case, the tuppences for going were very welcome to the youthful entrepreneurs. Coke came from the corporation yard, and was sold by the huge shovelful. You got a reasonable quantity in a bag for 4*d*. Many families never saw a bag of coal from the coalman, but relied on cinders, coke and the occasional quarter or half hundredweight of coal from the coal yard.

Looking back, I feel surprised and pleased at the amount of tolerance shown towards each other's funny little ways, considering that life was hard, money short and jobs hard to get. If some people behaved in ways you would not care to emulate, at least they seldom interfered with each other.

As I grew older and saw other working-class districts, I felt sorry for the people living in the usual monotonous grid of Lancashire industrial housing, house facing house across the narrow street, back entries parallel to each other, no variety anywhere. Empire Street was nothing like that. It was an interesting shape to begin with, having a right-angled bend at one end. And although the thirty-six houses on our side were all alike, there was a row of four so-called garden houses (or rather the 'gardin 'ouses' in local parlance) on the other side. These four houses had two foot of garden at most, with very little in the way of plant life.

Nevertheless, these gardens were railed off and were thus a class apart from Empire Street, with its little houses opening straight onto the pavement. We didn't socialise with the residents of the garden houses, one of whom was the local bookie. We took our fathers' 'sixpence each way' betting slips round the back.

The rest of the street frontage was lined with assorted factories. From the 'pan end' at the other end of the street there was the African mill, with its extreme heat and noise, the Shell petrol depot sporting signs saying 'No Smoking, No Matches, No Lights Allowed', the rubber works, the toffee works, the mill and the chemical works. I don't remember much about the chemical works, beyond my infantile puzzlement on hearing that the workers were 'playing' two days a week [i.e. working a three-day week].

In the summer, office girls at the mill propped the doors open with a wedge of coloured blotting. Local children would pinch it, attracted by the different colours. You could go up five floors of fire escapes to watch the machines at work. We used to pinch the cops [spindles] out of the skips to play with.

The local outdoor market was treated as if it was the only one of its kind. The nearest main road, well stocked with shops, was never called anything but The Road. We had never heard of the expression 'the definite article', but we used it liberally. As a small child I firmly believed that only one of each of these places existed. In my childish mind there was only one canal, one park, one chip shop. All of which helped to tie me more firmly to our street and its immediate environs.

At the top end of Empire Street was the croft, a large, open cinder-surfaced area, partly covered with an assortment of huge industrial ships' boilers awaiting repair. This, together with easy access to the canal, and the park only five minutes away, represented a freely available adventure playground, of which we children made full use. The boiler works was next to the croft and spread its cinders there. This had a great many benefits for us local children, quite apart from Saturday football matches and dirt-track racing on old bicycles.

The ships' boilers were all large ones. The flat ones made wonderful stages for step-dancing and such, and the enclosed ones with small entrances gave endless opportunities for climbing and jumping. Nobody ever told us to run away and play. I suppose there was very little damage kids could do to these rusting monsters.

Our long row of terraced houses was roughly divided down the middle into 'our end' and 'the other end'. I don't know if the 'other enders' had their own complementary version of this nomenclature, but their children tended to do their own thing as a rule. That is, unless we happened to be playing a particularly jolly game, when all requests to join in were granted without argument. With so much of the street frontage lined with factories, great stretches of unappropriated pavement were left for us children to play on. And play on it we did, without needing to watch out for irate housewives telling us to go and play outside our own homes. The factory side of Empire Street had no newly donkey-stoned patches on which you dared not walk, let alone play hop-flag [hopscotch].

There was a grocery shop at each end of our row, a small one and a much larger one which was also an off-licence.[2] Insofar as we dealt with any shop in particular, we patronised the larger shop which in any case was nearer to us. The corner shop sold nearly everything except fresh meat. Potatoes were kept in huge skips. People were always dropping money into them, which caused great annoyance.

The smaller shop at the bottom end was run by an old lady called Alice Greaves. Her shop did not have as big a choice as the other one, but in her favour she would sell small quantities: a saucerful of jam or pickles, a gill of milk, two ounces of tea and so forth. She kept her milk supply in a beautiful white china pail with the measures hanging over the side. I greatly admired this container, though it was very seldom that I was sent for anything from its china depths. We used mostly condensed milk. If on some special occasion liquid milk was needed, we went to our own nearer corner shop for a bottle of 'cow-milk'.

Some people bought 'Stera' sterilised milk, but my mother disapproved of it and wouldn't have it in the house. You could of course leave a jug on the doorstep and have milk delivered, but this was out of our range. Other items were often bought from street vendors who had their regular street cries. We were used to being sent out to see if we could see or hear 'colly-olly' from the man with the vegetable barrow, 'one and six a bag, good house coal', 'rag, bone, donkey stones, cream stones, white stones, four a penny', 'all the latest songs, one penny' and so on.[3] The ragman also sold soap of all kinds: white and brown Windsor, carbolic and mottled. We used only white Windsor and carbolic soap. This last was a green soft soap in its own container.

Even our front street, the cart road, as the stone-set roadway was always called, had very little traffic, and most of that was horse-drawn lorries and handcarts. Your average ragman, trading in the front street with a low handcart, had to contend with stubborn housewives who persisted in pegging out the washing across the front street, citing immemorial custom.[4] These chaps got away with it because their small carts only required a hand to lift a sheet to let them through, but there were often flaming rows with drivers of large wagons. For handcarts and such, a polite request would produce a prop to raise the wash line sufficiently to make a temporary passage.

The railings of the local central school ran parallel with the back entries of our row of houses. These back lanes enabled dustbins to be emptied on a set day, and smaller items to be pegged out there on washdays. Drivers of larger vehicles had a harder time, having to contend with noisy rows and long delays. The occasional coalman, calling on the 'wrong' day, was lucky to get away with a whole skin after a heated altercation. The growing popularity of the corporation wash-house, with its electric machines, the giant whizzer, and drying racks to finish off, finally saw an end to these minor episodes of street theatre, which were meat and drink to the local children. Everybody loved a good row.

Better than the 'Mind that washin'!' scuffles were the real shouting matches in the street, when one or more of the participants had 'had a few'. 'Bashing up' was even better, but Empire Street was not a very violent street. Large families with six or seven kids were the rule. As many as eighteen people were known to live in a single two-bedroomed house.

Street buskers were quite a common sight on Friday nights and at the weekends. 'Where Is My Wandering Boy Tonight?' was a sure-fire winner if you knew where to go with it. We saw a lot of 'Charlie Chaplins', etc. People were glad to see them if they were any good at all.

There were, I think, thirty-six houses in our row in Empire Street. They were all identical in construction, with the same four rooms and the same facilities: gas, cold water and an outside toilet. All were two-up and two-down terraced houses, but no two homes were precisely alike, inside or out. Each family stamped its personality on its own dwelling. The outsides of the Empire Street houses didn't offer much scope for personalisation. The front door was painted by the landlord, if at all, because of course they were all rented. There were two windows, which did at least give a choice of lace curtains or a blind.

There were casement curtains which you could close at night, and the best sham [artificial] blind if you could afford it across the top. If you were fussy about people looking in, there would be a semi-transparent stick-on material across the lower sash. However, this did not exhaust the possibilities of individualism. There was always the 'stoning' of the flags and the window sill.[5] From my memories of the procedure of stoning, I see it as a much neglected folk art form. No two designs were the same in colour or pattern. How we despised fronts with a lot of plain white, for example.

Girls had to be carefully initiated into the family tradition as soon as they were old enough. The donkey stones came in white, cream and brown. We used all three colours, and I can almost convince myself that I could do it now if it were possible. The ritual included wetting the flags with a thick mop-rag, wringing it out and partially drying the surface. Then, in our case, we applied a carefully controlled squiggle of each colour. This was then blended with the wrung-out rag into a delightful café-au-lait shade, before we proceeded to the window sill to give it a final, tasteful touch of a very fine edging of pure white.

The backyard was also stoned (although not in our case) with just a plain cream border round the edges. Some people stoned the whole of the surface in their yards, and then would not let the children play on it. This caused a lot of comment in the street, when anyone managed to get a glimpse through a seldom-opened yard door. It was rumoured that a few people had plants in their yards, but I never saw any.

One disadvantage of the street was the knackers' yard, next to the boiler works. Appalling smells emanated from this yard, especially in hot weather. We never ventured far inside this establishment, unless word had got round that there was a dead horse to be seen, whereupon we hung around the entrance until we got a glimpse of the poor creature – we thought of it as having grinning teeth – and fled immediately. This could be rather upsetting, but it was certainly a thrilling shock when a dead horse lay visible from the gateway, its teeth bared hideously. There was a tram stop [on Ashton New Road] a few yards further on, but no one ever seemed to board or alight there. The tram conductors, or guards as we always called them, called out 'Lavender Avenue' facetiously. This nickname was so hated that Empire Streeters preferred to get off at the previous stop and walk the extra distance, rather than be associated with the obnoxious smell.

On the opposite side of Empire Street to the croft, there were two short streets, Sidney Street and Herbert Street. They led into a square of waste ground which ran alongside the canal. The canal itself did not figure much in feminine recreations, although boys would often swim in it in the summer, irrespective of the dead dogs which were a common sight there. The thing for girls to do was to wait for a suitable barge and cadge a lift as far as the lock gates a few hundred yards ahead. This was strictly forbidden by most parents, but such prohibitions were generally disregarded, on the grounds that what the eye does not see, the heart cannot grieve over.

I suppose nowadays school pupils might be asked for essays on the effect of living in a street containing a chemical works, a knackers' yard, a boiler repair works, two cotton mills, a rubber works and a toffee works, but we never got much further than Alfred and the Cakes, and the Triumph of the Empire.

# 10

# *Gibbon Street Today*

Gibbon Street was a terraced street in a heavily indus-trialised part of East Manchester. Although the houses have now all gone,[1] Gibbon Street itself remains and is now the road leading to the Eastlands Asda hypermarket and to Manchester's magnificent National Cycling Centre. This is highly appropriate. When Nellie was a lass, the local lads used to race their bikes on a cinder track just off Gibbon Street. Her future husband Stan also took part in this dangerous sport.

The greater part of Gibbon Street was taken up with mills, factories and workshops. Years later, Nellie drew a remarkably accurate map of her street, which ran from Mill Street to Ashton New Road, enclosing a small triangular slice of Manchester life. The north side of Gibbon Street, which backed onto the Manchester and Ashton-under-Lyne canal, was almost all factories. From Mill Street, now replaced by Alan Turing Way, there was the Philips Park printing works and the Africa mill. Then there was the Shell Mex can depot, and the Wellington & Co. demolition yard. Next was Broadhurst & Co., rubber goods manufacturers, and a wireworks, a subsidiary plant of the Bradford ironworks. This was followed by the Bradford cotton mill of Robert Marsland & Co., cotton spinners, where Nellie's mother Ada and Ada's sister Lena both worked. Next came two small terraces, Sidney Street and Herbert Street, which led to the canal where Nellie's sister Annie drowned aged three.

Next were the four garden houses, in one of which the bookie lived. He was most likely Matthias Whittaker of 31 Gibbon Street. His house was next to the Little Croft, and three large chemical factories were on the other side of this open area.

The first was the soap works, officially the Tower chemical works of F.C. Calvert & Co. On the corner with Ashton New Road was the Manchester Chemical Co. Ltd and the Clayton Aniline Works. On the south side coming from Mill Street there were two small terraces, separated by a warehouse and a coal yard. The former was the Townley Works of G. Barnes & Son Ltd, manufacturing confectioners (the toffee works). Nellie's row of houses lay between the connecting streets of Queen Street and Sloane Street. In between the two shops at either end, there were thirty tiny terraced houses, Nos 26–84, which were all rented. Mrs Alice Greaves had the little shop, Nos 22/4, owned, it would seem, by Joseph Stock. Timothy Barnshaw was the proprietor of the main corner shop at Nos 86–90. Nellie lived at No. 76 Gibbon Street, five doors up from the shop.

Behind that section of Gibbon Street lay the Central School. The local elementary school and the chip shop were close by. Both were in Sloane Street, the chippie on the end house (No. 9) run by Albert Bradbury, who also owned No. 3 Sloane Street. One of the factories in nearby Corbett Street, A. Bradley Ltd, made chip-shop ranges and fish-frying equipment. Between Sloane Street and Upper Dover Street lay the open area known as the Croft, which was big enough to accommodate a soccer pitch. As on the north side, two more works led to Ashton New Road. The first was the boiler works of Topping Bros Ltd, then finally the bane of Gibbon Streeters, the abbatoir or slaughter yard. This was the premises of Dean & Wood Ltd, described as manure manufacturers. I presume this was a bone mill, where the bones of the slaughtered animals were ground up for fertiliser. The smell was so bad that Gibbon Street was sarcastically referred to as 'Paradise Row'.

The north side of Ashton New Road, from Mill Street to Gibbon Street, consisted mainly of houses and shops. All have now gone. On the corner with Mill Street stood the United Hotel, named after Manchester United, whose players used to change there before walking round to the ground at Bank Street.

Mary Griffiths was the licensee in 1935. Along this section of Ashton New Road were grocers' shops, drapers, florists, bootmakers, dining rooms, off-licences, a cycle dealer, dry cleaners, a radio and wireless dealer, a fruiterer, a watch repairer, a clothes shop, a medical herbalist and a tobacconist's. A Methodist chapel stood on the corner with Queen Street.

In 1935, Philips Park, at the top of Mill Street, boasted refreshment rooms and reading rooms, as well as three houses for the head gardener, Arthur Foster, and two of his staff. Edward Langton, the lock-keeper, lived by the canal. The three priests of St Brigid's parish, Frs Joseph Fitzgerald, Thomas Hourigan and John Hartley, lived in Mill Street, as did music teacher Miss Edith Bebbington AVCM. The Bradford Hotel, on the corner of Mill Street and Wilson Street, still stands. Harry Corner ran it in 1935.

It was the prospect of jobs in Manchester's abundant mills and factories that drew hundreds of thousands of Irish people like the Mapes to emigrate there. From 1801 to 1901, the population of Manchester grew from 70,000 to 544,000. It was not just Gibbon Street, the whole of Manchester's Bradford district was a hive of industry. Across the other side of Mill Street was a coal mine, Bradford Colliery, with its own link to the canal that served the businesses on the north side of Gibbon Street. The colliery, once the deepest in England, continued working until 1968. Across the canal stood the huge Stuart Street electricity power station, its six massive water-cooling towers dominating the landscape. In 1919, the year Nellie was born, it was the most powerful electricity-generating unit in the UK. There were ironworks, wireworks, leadworks, brickworks and a bakery. The whole area was criss-crossed with railways and their attendant bridges and viaducts. Nearby railway stations were Miles Platting, Park and the Beswick Goods station. Churches, chapels, schools, cinemas and shops, as well as the houses packed in everywhere, made up the mix that was Manchester life then. However, the Bradford area was an extremely unhealthy place to live.[2]

The Manchester and Ashton-under-Lyne canal cut diagonally across Mill Street and Ashton New Road, creating a small, distinct triangle of Manchester life. As a little girl, this triangle, cut off by two main roads and the canal, was Nellie's whole world. Gibbon Street, her street, also ran between the two busy roads, in parallel with the canal, and was thus the spine of the area. There were a dozen streets in all, with hundreds of tiny terraced houses and perhaps as many as 2,000 residents crammed into this small triangle of land along with numerous mills, factories, depots, workshops, shops, schools and churches.

Nowadays, this whole area is occupied entirely by a single retail development: the vast Asda superstore, a MacDonald's and several huge car parks. The main 180,000-sq ft Asda store, which took just thirty-three weeks to build, was opened in June 2002 and attracts an average 9,000 shoppers a day. The United Hotel, which stood on the corner of Mill Street and Ashton New Road at the very apex of Nellie's world has gone, along with all the rest. Manchester City's magnificent new stadium stands on the site of the former Bradford Colliery, across Alan Turing Way which has replaced the north–south axis of Mill Street.

The canal is still there, along with the lock-keeper's house, which is dated 1865. There are still traces of the mills and factories which fronted Gibbon Street and backed onto the canal. Portions of the railway viaduct which crossed the canal are still there. The Derby Arms, on the corner of Bank Street, is still going strong. Philips Park continues to provide recreation for young and old. Although some of the facilities have gone, the park has a thriving Friends group. The area south of the east–west link of Ashton New Road, where Nellie first went to work as a fourteen-year-old, is still a hive of industry.

Stan's diary records:

16 OCTOBER 1949

House in Gibbon Street for sale at £200. Property condemned twelve or more years ago, but good thing for crafty guy, who knows that, if house is pulled down in the future, corp will have to find him a council house.

In fact, most houses in Gibbon Street (including No. 76) remained until the mid-1960s when they were demolished along with most of the traditional terraced streets in the Bradford district. Just as superstores have replaced the corner shops, privately owned semi-detached houses and apartments have sprung up in place of the tightly packed rows of two-up two-down rented terraced homes. And, of course, the way we live now, with the emphasis on the individual and the nuclear family, is so different from the extended families and communal living of Nellie's day.

Poverty, widespread ill health and mass unemployment between the wars meant that people had to help one another just to get by. Clearly, we have gained massively in overall improvements in health, welfare and standard of living in the past seventy years, but at the same time what have we lost? Nellie had similar sentiments when she visited her old stamping ground in her later years:

I recently took a stroll down Empire Street. Reflecting on the fact that the centre of my own local town remains in memory as it was, more like a museum model than a street map, I had decided to visit the street where I was born. By now the houses had gone, and the site where each house had stood looked remarkably small. It would appear that Gibbon Street is now Corbett Street. The pub has vanished. What was the knackers' yard is now a giant DIY store. There is no sign of the chemical works. Several small firms are now in residence, with some units to let. The croft is now occupied by Francis Shaw's social club, with its immaculate bowling green, etc.

Herbert Street is still a cobbled road off Sidney Street which also still remains, but without being named. Gibbon

Street resumes at Sloane Street. What was the fire hole of the mill now houses a car spares firm. The sites of the terraced houses and of the Central School have been grassed over. Queen Street and Princes Street are still there. Queen Street is now Quixall Street, while Princes Street is not named. Barnmouth Strcct Baths is virtually unchanged, although this establishment no longer offers hot tubs, only foot showers. The park (Philips Park), which was opened on 22 August 1846, now has no paddling pond, no bandstand and no swimming pool. Such is progress.

# 11

# *Love and Romance*

It was 4.30 p.m. on Boxing Day, 26 December 1937 when Nellie and Stan met for the first time. He was playing the piano, the tune 'I Want to Be Happy'. Nellie never forgot, and she did make Stan happy for the rest of his life. This is an extract from Nellie's ledger entitled 'New Men – owned & compiled by Nellie Mape': '26.12.37 New Man No. 106, Stan Wood, 21 Belgrave Road CHO 1107'. Stan told her, 'No one calls me Stanley. It's a horrid name. Just Stan'll do.' The question is, who were the other 105 men Nellie took an interest in before she met Stan? And what about the 'old' men? Sadly, the ledger itself has not survived, despite Nellie's hoarding instincts. Assuming she started it when she began work at the age of fourteen, that was a hundred men in just over four years – about one a fortnight. Nellie must have met a lot of men!

We do know that Nellie's first real passion with a member of the opposite sex was for 'Frank Number Three', a workmate. He came from a better-class home, just like Stan. He was 'tall, slim and fair-haired', as was Stan. And he was a piano player, just like Stan. But, like Frank Number One and Frank Number Two, this was strictly a one-sided affair. The teenage Nellie at first worshipped her men from afar (well, not too far away) and kept her passion to herself, other than following them home after work! No doubt many men whose names were recorded in Nellie's ledger came into this category. But there were others who were brought closer to Nellie through her favoured recreational activities: walking, camping, dancing and going to the theatre and the cinema. By the age of seventeen, Nellie was out almost every night.

Many young people of this era who had little money to spend but who wanted to go out and enjoy themselves in company did so by going walking and camping. At weekends, and even during the week in the lighter months, young men and women would travel out into the countryside by bicycle, bus or car, and go for walks. This activity – the healthy exercise in the fresh air, enjoying nature in a happy group – was in tune with many of the political trends of the day. The Juvenile Rechabites and the Young Communists, both organisations of which Nellie was a passionate and committed member, were just the sort of groups for which a planned walk in the countryside was an ideal activity for their relatively impoverished members.

Nellie liked music, she liked dancing and she liked dressing up. As well as the scores of dance halls in the Manchester area, there were the churches and social clubs who put on dances and other events for their members' enjoyment as well as to raise funds, much more than they do today. Nellie enjoyed the company of young men. She was a very attractive young woman and never lacked for male company. She was also strong-minded and outspoken, and would not have allowed any liberties. Any male making unwanted advances would be given short shrift.

Most of all, Nellie enjoyed going to the pictures and to the theatre. At the age of seventeen she was going to films and shows three or four times a week, as well as attending temperance and political meetings, marching and canvassing. Most nights she would be in the company of one or more of her young men, and just occasionally on her own. She rarely stayed in. In 1937 Harry Winstanley seems to have been a regular date, until she jilted him. She was 'in seventh heaven' on a bench at the camp-site with Barney, but walked back 'in fourteenth heaven', presumably with two blokes! Eric Bland stood her up, so Nellie fixed to go on a ramble with Tom. Then Nellie met Stan.

This is Stan's potted history of himself, as he wrote it in January 1983: 'Born 1912 in Salford. Educated Chorlton High

School 1924 to 1928, Went into insurance 1929 to 1935. Ran own dance band and was freelance journalist until 1941 when joined Navy. Lieutenant RNVR, Editor of Naval Magazine *Guzz*. 1946 to 1950 Liberal Agent in Bury. Wrote several radio plays including radio musical *The Story of Sylvia Morris* produced by Norman Swallow. Novel published by Hurst & Blackett *Death on a Smoke Boat*.[1] Stage musical *Clogs!* based on John Ackworth's *Clogshop Chronicles*, produced at Duke's Playhouse, Lancaster, and at Oldham Coliseum, and now going into repertory.' Much has been left out of this short CV, including Stan's successful wartime theatre productions and his time as a scriptwriter on *Coronation Street*.

In 1931 the Old Chorltonians Dramatic Society in Manchester put on a programme of two plays and two sketches. The first play was *Uncle Willy*, a farce in one act by Stanley Wood, who is also listed as a committee member of the Old Chorltonians Association. Stan was also chairman of the dramatic society and a member of the cast-selection committee. In March 1932 the society put on Stan's play *The Riddle of Randle*. Stan was just nineteen years old. In the meantime, in another part of Manchester, Nellie was musing about love:

> When I was a girl I often asked myself, what would 'falling in love' involve? How would you know when it had happened? What would it feel like? My prolific reading of trashy novels, as well as Dickens, Brontë & Co. in my early teen years, fostered the idea of a miraculous golden glow unmistakable in its nature and effects. In my last year at school I was useful to the teachers for running errands, and for taking messages across to the boys' school. This was a sought-after chore, but all jealousy among my schoolmates disappeared when one teacher was overheard saying to another, 'The boys won't whistle after her, at any rate!'
>
> Up to the age of eighteen, I had never fallen for any male person in 'that sort of way'. I did have more than one crush

on selected older chaps in the factory where I worked, but these were, and essentially had to be, out of my reach. The object of my affection invariably already had a 'young lady' of his own, and a life outside the factory totally unknown to me. Three of my early attachments were all called Frank. Frank Number One, the earliest of these unattainable creatures, was dark-haired and handsome. He was aged nineteen, and had to get married soon after our acquaintance began. I asked one of the older men why did he have to get married if he didn't want to, to which he only replied 'circumstances', and I was no further on.

The second of these crushes, Frank Number Two, was not so handsome. In my view he was very intelligent, although I can't remember on what I based this assessment. My relationship with him centred around the quarter of sweets I bought every Friday after I got my wages, and the 'accidental' encounter on the way home. Frank Number Two would always accept a humbug or a caramel from me and eat it in my presence.

Frank Number Three was the joy of my teenage life. He was tall, slim and fair-haired. He worked in the inspection department at our factory, wore a khaki coat instead of overalls, and played the piano in his local Labour club. If I could get the right moment to be just about to slide back the heavy exit door from the workshop as he and his mates were leaving, they seemed to have no objection to my tagging along for part of the way home. I say 'seemed' because presumably a fourteen-year-old girl, silent though she may have been, could not have been a particularly welcome companion to a bunch of young men at the end of a hard day's work.

These occasions were absolute bliss to me, as were all occasions of contact with dear Frank. I idolized him, and he never let me down. He had, of course, a 'young lady'. I never met her, but I always pictured her, rightly or wrongly, dressed in her Sunday best, hatted and gloved as she came to a meat tea at Frank's house every Sunday. This social practice I discovered via the friendly older men in the workshop. These older men took a great interest in my (non) love affairs. They were constantly asking me if I had got my feet under the table yet, this to be the lead-up to the courting, engagement and marriage programme, none of which interested me in the slightest.

All good mothers liked to inspect their son's girlfriends, and Sunday tea was the accepted route to further acquaintance. But, the idea of any kind of conventional, possibly permanent, relationships frightened me, and I soon put a stop to any such development by a swift change of partners. Still, there was always Frank Number Three. I had the run of the workshops, and could always find an excuse to carry along some vital piece of paperwork in order to glance through his office window and get his never-failing smile. If ever there was a golden boy lighting up in my life it was then, between fourteen and sixteen. When a tall, blond, piano-playing man [Stan Wood] entered my world a couple of years later, it was no wonder I was set for life, although I didn't grasp that at the time.

One miserable winter day, there was no Frank! He was at home with flu. Talk about the sun having gone down, and 'keeps raining all the time', as the song said. Then what happened? Loudly, general manager to foreman: 'Send that office girl to get the key for the inspection cupboard.' The absence of this vital key had just been reported as the origin of some irritating hold-up in the workshop. There was the implication that Frank ought to have avoided getting flu, or at least made arrangements to send in the key. This later proved to be the case when I rang the bell (yes, they had a bell!) outside Frank's respectable terraced home.

His equally respectable mother explained that Frank was worrying about the key (dear Frank, perfect as always), but she was waiting in for the doctor, and couldn't bring it herself. She would get it for me. My feelings of importance were indescribable, but when she said, 'Would you like to go up and see him?' I nearly fainted. She said, 'go up', indicating the steep stairs stretching ahead of me from the front passage. Now, in my sphere of life, strangers never went upstairs in other people's houses; it just wasn't done. To be invited to visit a young man, any young man, in his bedroom (!) seemed incredible to me. But to see Frank! I couldn't believe it and nearly declined.

'Go on, it's all right,' she said encouragingly. Was she aware of who I was? I afterwards wondered. 'First on the left at the top.' I trod those carpeted stairs as if ascending to paradise, which of course I was. I glanced into the bathroom through its open door (hot and cold water, ooh!), then entered the bedroom. There was my Frank, an angel, a vision in pale-blue pyjamas.

I can scarcely recall what we talked about in our brief interview, but his welcoming smile said everything. He gave me several useful messages to take back, as well as the key. 'Trust Frank,' said his mates on receipt of same. His mother gave me a glass of milk and a half-coated digestive biscuit. I wished I'd had the courage to keep the biscuit as a memento, but that wouldn't have been polite. It was a hard job for the little girl (five feet tall) from Empire Street to pick up these minor points of social behaviour. Eventually Frank Number Three left our factory and found another job. I arranged to be 'accidentally' passing his new place of work as he came out, and offered him a toffee, bought specially to suit his taste.

An unwanted young admirer, Buster, however, was not to my taste at all. For one thing, he was not old enough for me to dote on, and his persistent doglike devotion irritated me extremely. The men were always singing his praises. According to them, Buster was practically a genius. I knew that he carried off all the prizes at night school, and that the bosses thought very highly of him. Buster was a bird watching, nature-loving youth. One Monday morning he brought me a pair of baby rabbits, which I refused to accept. Another day he brought me a hedgehog. He had just put it through the window of the office where I worked when the approach of the 'big boss' was semaphored by one of the drillers in the machine shop.

Buster fled. I hurriedly stuffed the poor animal into the bottom drawer of my desk, hoping it would not eat any vital papers, nor otherwise misbehave itself. The boss was in the office for about half an hour, receiving what were optimistically called progress reports. Sounds such as those made by a hedgehog scrabbling round in a drawer full of papers are not usually heard in office life, but we escaped with only a few blank looks, and an even deeper tone of purple on the managing director's cheeks. I imagine he could not lower himself to notice such an incredible noise.

We called the little creature Buster, and it seemed quite happy in our Victorian coal-hole under the stairs at home. Until one day, as hedgehogs do, it left home without notice to see the world. I never got another hedgehog, as the human Buster was warned by his foreman never to bring another animal into the workshop. The story went that the boss had needed half a bottle of whisky the day my hedgehog came.

Edible presents came mostly from a man considered by me to be practically in his grave – he must have been about forty! Novelty sweets were his speciality: sugar mice, smoker's outfits, sugar lockets and lucky potatoes. He was a bachelor, and followed a football team around every Saturday. When he tracked down something he had not given me before, in some obscure corner shop on his Saturday trips, he could hardly wait to get to my window with it on Monday morning.

A common practice for young people to pair up was called the 'monkey run'. Even so, very few boasted about it, and we tended to speak scornfully of those who did. The thing to do was to attach oneself as soon as possible and make up a four for cinema visits, park strolls, etc. 'Picking up' was not really socially acceptable, except among the less acceptable gals. People talked about the monkey run but very few admitted to going there. If you did go, and did pick up satisfactorily, the thing to do was to make up a four for walks and visits to the cinema for as long as the arrangement lasted.

Girls who were never seen on the monkey run despised the regular patrons, and refused approaches to make up a pair to go 'on spec', even to meet a specified couple of youths. To be asked to make up a pair to meet two lads, say, outside a cinema (the expression 'blind date' being then unknown) was a different matter. It was quite acceptable. Every youth seemed to have a pal, for whom a newly met girl acquaintance was required to bring a friend. Even so, these arrangements seldom lasted very long.

I had no experience of dance halls myself until the late 1930s, with the Ritz. Older girls used to talk of the dancing craze of the twenties, and how they used to get home from the mill, wash a dance frock, iron it partially dry and set off in damp garments hoping for a wonderful evening and the opportunity to 'click' with a young man. Some people simply did not care what other people thought of them. There were the grown-up girls from one family in Harold Street, who wore V-necked blouses 'showing the nick'.

The position of the houses in Empire Street, with only a back entry between them and the Central School lane, offered an ideal grandstand view over the schoolyard perimeter wall from the back bedrooms. This was not terribly interesting to us children, but was much appreciated by unemployed fathers and brothers. With time on their hands, the men delighted in watching the gymslipped maidens at their netball practice. They particularly appreciated the similarly clad, but more well-built figure of the PE teacher, who was equally active and so put on a better show.

## Extracts from Nellie's Diary

### 1937 – Nellie aged seventeen

JANUARY 1937

1st  Breakfast at Harry Winstanly's. Home to dinner, then Hillkirk St Fair: Harold Winstanly's for tea, then to Casino, *The Singing Kid*. Winstanly's for supper.

2nd  Hippodrome with Harry Winstanly, *Robinson Crusoe*.

3rd  Walk with Eric Bland.

4th  Shaftesbury, *Ex Mr Bradford* with Eric Bland.

5th  Stayed in.

6th  Rivoli, *Till We Meet Again* with Eric Bland.

7th  Grand, *The Princess Comes Across* with Eric Bland.

8th  Stayed in.

9th  The King's, *The Walking Dead* with Harry Winstanly.

10th  Fred Winstanly's house with Harry.

11th  Queen's, *Tudor Rose* with Harry.

12th  Stayed in.

13th  Arcadia, *It's Love Again* with Harry.

14th  Rivoli, *Kelly the Second* with Harry.

15th  Stayed in.

16th  Queen's, *East Meets West* with Harry.

17th  Fred Winstanly's house with Harry.

18th    Arcadia, *Laughing Irish Eyes* with Harry.
19th    Stayed in.
20th    Queen's, *Under Two Flags* with Harry.
21st    Circus with Harry.
22nd    Stayed in.
23rd    Concert, Wesley Hall with Harry.
24th    Unity Meeting, Free Trade Hall (didn't see Barney).
25th    Joan's place for tea. Challenge Canvass.
26th    Shaftesbury, *Sutter's Gold* with Harry.
27th    Stayed in.
28th    Rivoli, Sabotage and *House of 1,000 Candles* with Harry.
29th    Rechabite Juvenile Meeting.
30th    King's, *Hot Money* with Harry.
31st    Fred Winstanly's house with Harry.


FEBRUARY 1937

1st     Grand, *Mr Deeds Goes to Town* with Harry.
2nd     Stayed in.
3rd     Stayed in.
4th     Council Meeting, Juvenile Rally and Cinema. Alone.
5th     Dance. Victoria Hotel. Met Frank Heathcote. Alone.
6th     Metropole, *Variety* with Harry.
7th     Fred's house with Harry.
8th     Queen's, *All In* with Harry.
9th     Stayed in.
10th    Conservation Street Corner Meeting.
11th    Derby Street. Failure. Alone.
12th    Juvenile Rechabite Meeting, Cinema Show with John Wesley Tent.
13th    Queen's *Small Town Girl*, OK. Rec[eived] Valentine and chocs from Peter.
14th    Lyons Café. Walked home with Frank Heathcote.

15th   Repertory Theatre, *Little Women*. No good. Harry.
16th   Labour Party canvass, Far Lane. Walked past ESC,[2] saw Frank Nadin, Bill Girst and Harold Chant.
17th   Hattons [?] no go. Stayed in.
18th   Election canvass, Mr Benn Spoke. 'Red Flag' ['The Internationale'] sung.
19th   Rechabite Adult Meeting. Speaker Bro. M. Williams. Jolly good points. Prickly though.
20th   Corona, H.G. Wells's *Things to Come* with Harry.
21st   Fred's house. Stimulating discussion.
22nd   Shaftesbury, *Broken Blossoms*. Very good. Harry.
23rd   Walk, met Batty, went to Rose's house.
24th   Queen's, *Annie Laurie*. *Maria Martin*. Harry.
25th   Stayed in.
26th   Temperance Knowledge Exam. Rechabite Tent.
27th   *Little Lord Fauntleroy*. Splendid. Harry. Shaftesbury.
28th   Fred's House. Harry.

MARCH 1937
1st   Musical Festival Committee Meeting. J. Wiggins.
2nd   King's, *Show Boat*. Not Bad. Harry.
3rd   Ardwick, *Mutiny on the Bounty*, Frank Heathcote. Never again. Film disappointing.
4th   Council Meeting. Disappointing. J. Wiggins.
5th   Adult Rechabite Meeting. Visit of David's Glory Tent [Rechabites]. Returned with Cyril Beaumont.
6th   Musical Festival Rally. Returned with J. Wiggins.
7th   Fred's House alone. No boys – no gang.
8th   Shaftesbury, *Dracula's Daughter*. Not bad. Harry.
9th   Stayed in.
10th   Harry's house. Sorted music. Tried to play piano.
11th   Inaugurating social for Social Fellowship. Harry.
12th   Stayed in.
13th   King's, *Three Maxims*. OK. Harry.

14th   Bill Nicholson not in. Met Eddie Howell.

15th   Walk with Eddie Howell.

16th   Stayed in.

17th   Ardwick, *A Son Comes Home*. Not bad. Harry &
       Mrs W.

18th   Too late for Eddie Howell. Went for walk alone.

19th   Adult Rechabite Meeting. Met Bill Fox.

20th   Stayed in.

21st   Went on motorbike afternoon. Burnt leg. Fred's
       house. Harry, Emily and Jim.

22nd   Queen's, *Hard Rock Harrington*, *Guilty Melody*.
       OK.

23rd   Stayed in.

24th   Meeting. Saw Dr Goldie about burn. Saw
       Ashbrook for first time.

25th   Stayed in.

26th   Train to Glossop. Fairey's draughtsman. Grouse
       Inn. OK. Passed O's and Cyril. To Ashes. Joan,
       Kinder, Hayfield. Bus to Glossop and train home.

27th   Ramble to Harrop Edge with RSF rambling club.
       Got lost. Home with J. Wiggins.

28th   Stayed in, then went to Dolly's (Fred's wife). Acted
       the fool.

29th   Train to Marple. Walked across country with Bills
       and Dick. Scratched to death. Met Clarice Fisher's
       gang – rambled to Mottram. I like Ray Norman.
       Buchanan brought me home.

30th   Rivoli, *Hot Money*, *Murder in the Big House* with
       Bill Rice.

31st   Saw Eric Bland this morning and made a date.
       Olympia, *Dancing Pirate*. Not bad.

APRIL 1937

1st    Stormy Annual Council Meeting. J. Wiggins.

2nd    Stayed in.

3rd    Grand, *Keep Your Seats Please*. VG. Harry.

4th    Dolly's house. Emily, Jim and Harry.

5th    Dr Bourke about leg. King's, *Modern Madness*.
       Fair. *Homes Broken*. VG. Unknown British actor.
       Harry.

6th    Met Bill Fox waiting for me at lake entrance. Dr
       Bourke about leg (burn). Walk with Bill Fox.

7th    Stayed in. Altered navy jumper.

8th    Bill Fox let me down. Saw Dr Bourke about leg.

9th    Juvenile Rechabite Meeting. T. Hughes retiring.
       Talked about juvenile ramble to H. Taylor.

10th   Olympia, *Say It with Music*, *Marine Follies*, *The
       Champ's a Chump* (all seen before). Harry.

11th   Fred's. Jim, Emily, Harry and Dolly. Went home
       without Harry.

12th   Concert party.

13th   Concert party.

14th   Concert party.

15th   Concert party.

16th   Stayed in.

17th   Dance, Mill Street, Free Church.

18th   Winstanly's House.

19th   Concert party.

20th   Jilted Harry. Met nice chip-shop boy. Concert
       party.

21st   Concert party.

22nd   Interview, Palace. Let you know.

23rd   Interview, Palace. Got it.

24th   Lewis's [department store]. Cinema, 28s. *Any Old
       Port*, OK. *Accused*, OK.

25th   Walked. Met book boy. Also some of gang –
       walked on. Went to Winstanly's alone.

26th   Cinema, 11s. *Caught By Television* and
       *Blackmailer*. Both OK.

27th   Cinema, 13s.

28th    Cinema, 11/6. Met Norman Clague. Arrive Friday
        10.00.
29th    Cinema, 14/3. Met another Norman – not up to
        much. *Harbour Lights, Calling all Tars, Bullets and
        Ballots*. VG.
30th    Cinema, 25/11. New shoes. Norman came. Sat
        with me till ten, and took me home.

MAY 1937

1st     Cinema, 37/6. Moseley. Norman waited for me.
2nd     Demo. Seventh heaven. Saw everybody including
        Barney, who stayed with me. Learned of Killick's
        death. My second most dearly loved friend. Can
        never be replaced.
3rd     Cinema, 19/9. Elsie has left, so I am here for a bit.
4th     Disappointment with stock. Cinema, 13/4. Bobby
        comes up to scratch.
5th     Cinema, 9/6.
6th     Cinema, 12s.
7th     Cinema, 14/6.
8th     Cinema, 37s.
10th    Cinema, 19/6. Norman turns up in trousers.
11th    Cinema, 14/6. Went to town.
12th    Coronation Day. Spent the day in bed. Cinema,
        26s.
13th    Bought blanket. Cinema, 19/6 (a penny short).
14th    Cinema 24s. Norman again in trousers.
15th    Skipped pictures. Caught 6.14 train at Belle Vue.
        Met Henry at Hayfield and some of the boys. Went
        nearly to Glossop – met Joan, came back to Ashes,
        stayed the night.
16th    Went to camp at 1 o'clock – 'Bunny' shouted
        Barney. Went ramble. All got terribly wet, except
        me in my coat. Changed. Had tea with Barney. Met
        and liked Kathleen.

17th    Weather quite wet. Just sufficient to be with
        Barney. Caught 10.09 train. Saw Joan, Mick,
        Henry and Ben. Alighted at Ashbury's. Met Dolly
        and went home with her.

18th    Stayed in. If I go to the cinema I get the sack, so
        resigned – more dignified.

19th    Stayed in.

20th    Winstanly's. Very hard up.

21st    Borrowed from Peter. Made preparations. Washed
        all things, still damp.

22nd    Caught 9.26 from Ashbury's. Arrived at camp at
        11.10, lounged till dinner. At 3.10 went to Glossop
        and sat on a bench in seventh heaven with Barney.
        Came back, had tea. Barney slightly cramped with
        stomach pains.
        Went to Grouse Inn with the others, walked back
        in fourteenth heaven.

23rd    Barney had cramps badly till dinner. Cancelled trip
        to Ashes because of rain. Barney's brothers came.
        Caught 8.09 train. Saw Fred Winstanly and went to
        their house.

24th    Went on walk, Gorton–Reddish
        Canal–Gorton–Openshaw, until too dark to read.
        Met J. Bell, Aldred and Les Armitage.

25th    To Challenge Club, saw Monty. Barney took me for
        a walk. Says he'll write to me.

26th    Went for ointment. Saw Ada and Alf and stayed in
        sewing.

27th    Film show at Athenaeum. Saw Barney and walked
        to car with him.

JUNE 1937

1st     Rec[eived] letter from Barney, suggests ramble. I
        accept, of course.

2nd     Ramble with Barney.

12th    Rivoli, *Gorgeous Hussy* with Eric Bland.

13th    Took Eric to Dolly's.

14th    King's, *Captain Kidd*, Alf.

15th    Corona, *Ben-Hur*, Eric Bland.

18th    Walk. Met D.T. Jones.

19th    Alhambra, *Gypsy King of the Ice Rink*, Eric Bland.

20th    Met Eric Dawson afternoon. Walk, Eric Bland, at night.

21st    Walk, Eric Dawson.

22nd    Walk, Dick Trevor Jones.

23rd    King's, *Gay Desperado*, Peter Cryne.

24th    Went for Eric Bland – not there. Saw Bill Fox till quarter to ten. Saw Ted and Tom Frost and fixed up a ramble for Sunday with Tom.

25th    Received a pound at Adult Meeting. Stanley Booth came to present it. I had to reply. [See Chapter 7, 'The Demon Drink'.]

# 12

# *Postscript*

Nellie kept all of Stan's wartime letters to her, and a huge number of these have survived, far too many to include in this book. Most of the small selection of Stan's letters I have included were written in 1939, the year before Stan and Nellie got married, and show how rocky and volatile their courtship was. Stan was all too aware of his own failings, but he was obviously passionately in love with Nellie. Stan begged her to take one or two evenings a week off from her political activities with the Young Communists to make some time for him. Stan was possessive and had traditional views about the man's role in a relationship, while the beautiful and independent-minded Nellie lectured him about the equality of the sexes. Stan blamed his emotional difficulties on being brought up as a solitary child with an absent father (fighting in the First World War) and a distant mother who kicked up her heels in Manchester while he was parked with his granny in rural Lincolnshire.

At one point, Stan says he is a rotten lover. Later he says he will break off their relationship unless Nellie changes her attitude. Both our parents were clever, intelligent, thoughtful and articulate, but the two were very different in their approach to life. Stan was all for getting round problems and smoothing things over with soothing words. He was a superb salesman and a great raconteur. Nellie would bluntly state her true feelings and would stick by what she said, no matter what. If things did not go her way, she would clam up. Once she had formed an opinion, nothing and no one could change it.

Although not specifically mentioned in the letters, one possible cause of friction between Nellie and Stan was the relationship between the two women Stan loved the most, Nellie and his mother Eleanor. It's hardly surprising that they didn't get on. Nellie was young, working class, anti-establishment and outspoken. Eleanor was middle-aged, middle class, and snobbish with pretensions of grandeur. Stan was her only child (she spoiled him rotten), and Nellie was definitely not the sort of wife that she had had in mind for her darling boy. Even as a small boy, I was aware of the tensions between the two women I, like my Dad, loved the most. Nellie had as little as possible to do with her mother-in-law, and Eleanor likewise with Nellie. I spent a lot of time with both my mother and my nana, and neither woman ever mentioned the other to me, not once.

One early Nellie–Eleanor clash happened like this. Eleanor had a telephone in the house – naturally – while there was no phone in Nellie's home or in her digs, so she had to phone from a call-box. One evening (the time is uncertain, but it was possibly about 9 p.m.) Nellie rang Stan's home in Chorlton-cum-Hardy. She asked for Stan. 'Whom may I say is calling?' asked Eleanor in her Lady Bracknell voice. 'It's Helen,' said Nellie, to which Eleanor replied in her best 'handbag' tones, 'Stanley is not at home. One does not expect a young lady to telephone a young gentleman at this hour. Kindly do not call again.' Without waiting for a response, Eleanor put down the receiver. Well, she crashed it down.

Eleanor was no doubt scandalised by the fact that Nellie was pregnant when she and Stan married in 1940. That was despite the fact that Eleanor herself was almost certainly pregnant with Stan when she married her husband John on 5 December 1911. Stanley was born on 1 July 1912, barely seven months later. As far as I am aware, it was not a premature birth. Stan was a good and loyal son to his mother, and in her later years he would visit her every day. There are almost always tensions with in-laws, but I have no doubt this particular clash caused Stan problems right from the start.

## Stan's Letters to Nellie

*[Written note on Stan's business card, circa 1938]*

Darling
I want you to use most of the enclosed to buy yourself a
present for me and put the balance towards any scheme we
have planned in the future.
All my love
Stan x
(Ma talks about you as 'that very nice girl'.)

*[Letter, c. 1939]*

Love
Your letter has spoiled a great plan my mighty brain was
evolving. I was going to meet you tonight at Victoria
[Manchester Station] as you came home from Blackburn.
However, I feel that you would wish me to write instead. It
is a good idea, too. Although we see each other fairly
regularly, there are things which are more easily exposed in
black and white rather than [spoken] words. On Tuesday
night, as I walked home, I was angry with you. I made up
my mind never to see you again. I was going to call off
Sunday. I was fed up with rowing and haggling and being
misinterpreted. 'She's as touchy as an old b—— hen,' I kept
saying to myself (just like a parrot).
    And I was fed up with smoking, drinking, laziness and
late hours. My eyes were bad and gave me constant
headaches, too (isn't the man a terrible child?). On
Wednesday, I had my four cigarettes, no ale, worked hard,
ate lots of salad and fruit, and slowly the disease went out
of my brain. At night, I saw Mick [a pal], and as I talked to
him about things, I found myself chattering away with all

the old enthusiasm (about you, of course). Then when I was in bed, something inside went very warm towards you. It is nearly always there (unless you get me mad), and I decided to forgive you (forgive what – I don't know), so I planned to meet you at the station and perhaps buy you a little present ('cept that I am broke).

In my mind I had drawn up a balance sheet of our affair, but previously I had only concentrated on the debit side. Now I saw the credit items in all their glory. And the truth is that the debit side is really only a reflection of an occasional 'bad days' feeling of self-dissatisfaction. I have achieved nothing – but everything. In politics – a no-good and rightly ostracised; in money – just in debt; in writing – nothing achieved really though I am slightly 'on the way'; home life – not very happy; material prospects – fairly good if I strengthen my morale. In real life – 100 per cent without a doubt!

Now don't – for the love of Mike – take on yourself the burden of any of these debit items. I'll clean 'em up, and they arise through my own faults entirely. (We are both weak characters, really, sweetheart. Never denying each other anything shows how big our love is – but it plays merry hell on occasions with more mundane matters!) Perhaps if we both had chins like battleships we should be better off – but, probably, less happy. Anyway, I am starting to grow one.

Now for the other side of the picture. Just let me comment on your letter. I disagree with your views on love – at the beginning of the letter – but I agree with the end. I think that that 'double-barrelled' way of thinking of yours is very dangerous and is not easy to understand – objectively. You end up by putting yourself in a false position – to others, if not as yourself. It is ridiculous for a woman to say, 'I love him so much that I will kill myself so's not to be a burden on him.'

When all is said and done, it takes two to make a partnership. Don't your arguments take into account my thoughts and feelings? I have been very happy this year and, mostly, you have been responsible for it. Of course I'm the world's worst egotist and so on, but when you try to please me (clothes, etc.) I feel very humble and small, wishing to dissolve into tears of love. There are times when I am conscious of your love shining through, like a pure brilliant light, so that I am ashamed of my own puny and shabby spirit.

You see, duck, I love you. More than that, I love you to the uttermost extent of which I am capable. But yours is bigger and better, and purer. I'm a bundle of complexes and inhibitions. My poor old love for you has to struggle through a welter of opposing ideas. You know some of them: my folks; my ridiculous idealism (almost a schoolboy's idealism); my old instinct of independence, and so on.

I told you how I grew up on my own. No brothers or sisters, father in Flanders, mother hundreds of miles away, no little lads to play with, a solitary child; and solitariness breeds its own antidote: a hardness, a mask, a disguise to show the world that it can't hurt me. Perhaps that is why on occasions I could be capable of almost incredible cruelty, particularly in emotionally hurting people. And above all that, my love for you has managed to rise and dominate.

The dark mists of egotism gone bad were not allowed, by your home life, to collect in your head. I still love to fight. One thing is war. Taking into account my mind and your mind, and although I said before that your love is better than mine, it is still true to say that I love you as much as you love me. Each loves in his own fashion.

I hope you like this letter, love. By the way, you wrote splendidly. That is understandable – for it came straight from you. Well so has this. I wish I was not so dependent on objectivity for my reactions. You would not feel any different about me if I was cross-eyed or bald or scarred, would you? I wish it was so noble in outlook . . . but honestly, you've no idea how I love to see you looking young and healthy and neat.

That's another example of how my love got a dint in it as it was passing through the mental mill. Somehow, a ruddy complexion or 'washerwoman' hair seems so very unfair – not that these things arise much these days (and you dress wonderfully well). Men are indeed the possessors of a 'peacock' sort of mentality.

For my own part I can't afford to dress as I much wish, but, quietly, I try to please you, and I get miserable if I am unduly grubby in your presence.

I think that is all, pro tem. I want you a good deal – and my bed is a lonesome place. However, there are green fields and woods, and maybe Mother Nature will cover us over with leaves like the babes in the wood.

All my love, darling, till Sunday at seven.
Stan
PS This letter is still a wee bit reserved, isn't it?
Never mind. I am slowly learning to be more fluent.
I'm really rather a poor sort of lover xxx.

*[Letter, c. 1939]*

Stanley Wood ACII
21 Belgrave Road
Chorlton-cum-Hardy
Manchester

Helen
Thanks for your letter. The directions are fairly clear and I will be down at the cottage at 5 p.m. prompt. The old

beeza [BSA motorbike] is being done up and it may not be ready in time, in which case I will send a telegram, but I hope our Albert will sort the machinery out speedily. The old eyes are a little better, although somewhat red, and a wretched cold is laying me low. Today I hope to be able to raise enough energy to totter off to Southport on some [insurance] claims.

My camera has a finished spool in it which I am taking out and then you can have it. Could you buy a film? It is the standard size, 2¼ × 3¼, I think. I hope you are having a good time, and don't forget to remind the RAF that in spite of the natty uniforms they still belong to the working-class – the men I mean, not the uniforms. Maybe you could get some *Daily Worker* readers?

By the way, do you know Kenneth Moore of Manchester? His name is in the list that has just come through in respect of those killed at Teruel. I rather think that he was in our branch. Well, I must be off to sunny Southport now. See you at 5 p.m. at Brook Houses.

Stan
PS No one calls me Stanley. It's a horrid name. Just Stan'll do.

*[Letter, September 1939]*

21 Belgrave Road
Chorlton-cum-Hardy

Love
Please don't read this letter until you're in the mood. Okay? Thanks. I was sorry we ended on rather a dismal note last night, particularly when things were so much brighter a short time before. Still, you said your little piece and I said mine and there's an end on't. I've been wanting

to phone you today but managed to avoid the old instrument, though I would have loved to speak to you. Still I have a complex about phoning during office hours.

You said some unkind things last night (my fault, probably), but I still disagree with you very much about £sd. When I have turned the corner, so to speak, I shall want to buy you things as I once said before, and I shall also want to pay when we go out anywhere. I agree with you about equality and, when circumstances permit, there is every reason why the bloke should be, shall we say, possessive.

I know I have been a swine as regards the point in question, and your attitude is quite justified. Even so, it is not fair of you if you maintain your attitude about paying every wretched halfpenny, and if you stick by your 'resolve' I shall be hurt about it. In fact, if you insist on maintaining that angle, when I am all straight (as I shall soon be) I will beat it for good. I mean that.

In the old days, when I contributed in a small way towards that coat, for example, I was tremendously bucked about it, more than you will ever know, and I want to be able to do the same sort of thing again in the future. Please don't forget all the things I said on that Tuesday night (the very nice night, remember?), I still mean them. So, love, will you forgive my nastiness and give my puny little ambitions a chance to come true?

I have a lot more in my head about the same subject, but in deference to your 'touchiness' we'll leave it at that. What I honestly feel is that if you and I will be only a little more tolerant and sympathetic towards each other, we can cut out altogether these wretched little differences which crop up from time to time. When all is said and done, we have had some very wonderful times together, such things as come to but few folk in a lifetime, and with care we can preserve it. It is worth the effort, don't you think?

Another thing: now that you are getting all stern and businesslike and terribly busy on Party work, we shall have to see that we don't get out of touch. I'm scared of getting an anti-woman mood on me, and it never arises without some fairly just reason. I don't want to think that I am less important to you than a dance at the Advance Club. You wouldn't like to think that you were less important to me than a night dictating stories to a girl typist. We owe a little time to each other.

I'm quite prepared to put commitments on one side for one or two evenings a week, however important they are, if it means seeing you. I think the Cause should spare us one evening at least. If you get tied up every night for weeks and weeks I shall be jealous, and just to assert myself I shall turn elsewhere, just to show the whole world that I don't care two hoots about Mape [Nellie] anyway. (The opposite is the case.)

So we shall have to go into it. I always looked upon Sunday as our day, but at the moment it is not. Of course, the international situation isn't so good. Perhaps we can go back to Sunday later. I do hope you like this letter. Because I said I didn't like writing letters (and it was quite true) I am making a special effort just for you. Just to pay myself out for saying an unkind thing. I wouldn't do it for anybody else.

There is another small point – let me say it in a little whisper – I was wondering if sometime I could do Party work with you. Jessop once asked me to join the YCL [Young Communist League]. I wonder, what do you think? Not much, I suppose . . . I shall be at the meeting tonight but I shan't see you unless it is from afar. I shall creep in very sheepish, like, and hide in a corner. You have won back your spurs, but I have yet to do it. I was going to ask you if I could take you home tonight, but I have no right to ask. In any case, there'll be worthier blokes around.

More bad luck. Our dance tomorrow night for the LBC at Cheadle has been cancelled. God knows what I shall do with myself. Get drunk or something. I detest being free on Saturday nights.

Is your birthday on the 7th or the 14th? I want to buy you a present or take you out. Will you please tell me? I know. It's the 14th. Okay. Well, I must get some work done now. I have a lot to do. Will you reply to this letter if you feel like it? Write when you are in a nice mood. I could do with a nice letter at the moment. I am in a very loving mood. I wish you were here. However, you aren't, so that is that, but I love you all the same, for better or wuss [*sic*].

Cheerio, Darling
Stan
PS I am having those photographs developed and printed. They should be very good.

[*Letter card to Miss Colleen Mape*]
358 Lower Broughton Rd, Salford.
Thursday 14 March 1940, 6.30 p.m.

You were so very nice to me today under trying circumstances that I have just stopped at a post office on the way to a dance job to say that I love you very much and you are a wonderful girl. I think you and I get on a treat and the sooner we are married the better. You are the only girl in the world who could handle a difficult egotistic neurotic bloke such as I.

Thank you
All my love
Stan or Wood xxx.

I was born on 15 December 1940, exactly nine months after this card was written. Forgive me for imagining I was conceived this very day. Stan and Nellie did get married four months later, on 11 July 1940, by which time I was well on the way – CFW.

Stan was certainly struck by Nellie. Years later, in 1963, he wrote in his diary: 'I raved about her wearing a polo-neck sweater in powder-blue – loved it – and she thought I was raving about the sweater being powder-blue and polo neck. It has taken twenty-five years [i.e. since 1938] for her suddenly to realise what the attraction was – curvaceous, plural attractions!

## Nellie's Letters to Stan

Stan joined the Navy in 1941. He wrote to Nellie almost every day, sometimes twice a day. While Nellie kept all of Stan's wartime letters to her, Stan kept very few of the letters Nellie sent to him, although she wrote just as many as he did. In August 1942, Stan was serving in the Royal Navy and was based at HMS *Collingwood*, near Gosport, Hampshire. They had just spent the weekend together. Son Christopher was twenty months old, but was already being taken to the pictures by his mother. Nellie had learned to type and was looking for a 'posh job'. Nellie seems to have been writing to Stan at least once a day, and Stan did much the same. Home for Nellie and son was a rented house at 8 Heathbank Road, Cheadle Hulme, Cheshire.

Home
Monday Noon, 24 August 1942

Hello Darling
This is me getting a bit of practice in for the posh job I'm going to get one of these days. Hope you got a seat, love, and had a good journey. Actually my typing speed is not so

bad considering that this machine is so awful. I have sent an advertisement to the *Stockport Advertiser* today describing myself quite untruthfully as an intelligent woman. I will pack up your gas mask immediately I have finished this letter, and also your cup, which was hanging on the shelf. The little lad does not seem to be fretting about you, he takes it for granted that you come and go. I am missing you but I am not by any means miserable.

Something tells me I am going to get fixed up this week with a suitable job. I certainly hope so, as it will ease finances considerably. I must say you are very economical. It must be very awkward for you, never having any money to spend, but I am the same, and I can't spare you any more, or you know I would. I'll send you a parcel on Thursday, so expect it on Friday, or more probably Saturday.

I think Christopher and I will go to the pictures this afternoon, if the film is any good. There doesn't seem much more to write now, darling, but I will write again soon, probably tonight.

Bye, bye, darling. See you next weekend.
Your ever loving wife xxxx
Thanks for a marvellous weekend, darling.

In June 1943, Stan had just been promoted to lieutenant (entitling him to first-class rail travel!) and posted to Devonport Naval Base, Plymouth. Nellie moved to Plymouth to be near her Stan, taking son Christopher with her. Their second child and first daughter Penelope was born in Plymouth in 1945. Nellie was already writing, and submitting her literary efforts for Stan's approval. She says the children (who were the others besides me?) need clothes for Whitsuntide.

Home,
Monday Evening, 7 June 1943

Dearest Husband

Only a line or two to let you know I haven't pegged out entirely. Thank you so much for phoning me yesterday. I felt very gay afterwards, and very sure of seeing you very soon. Of course I still am. I seem to have been very busy lately, sewing and whatnot, not to mention my literary efforts. Believe me, if you cross out most of it and rewrite the rest, you might have something fairly presentable.

I am definitely coming on the 2 p.m. train. It's due in at 6 o'clock or thereabouts, so I will wait on the arrival platform at Euston until you turn up unless I hear to the contrary from you. I will stay somewhere or other, I am sure. It will be nice to travel back together. I will have to get an excess, of course, and travel first class. Joyce has promised to get my ticket and two pairs of stockings for me. Both my navy and wine shoes will be repaired by the weekend, and my tweed overcoat will be cleaned. Also your flannels, which I will bring. I have not told the old folks that I am going, so when I do tell them it will all have been decided on the spur of the moment.

I am very busy getting ready, because it is Whitsuntide and the children must have something to wear, which further runs away with the cash. Never mind, we will get through all right.

I had better call it a day. If you need a decision and there isn't time to write, you can phone me any night. Meantime, you can confirm this: Saturday next, Euston, meet the 3 p.m. train from Manchester on the arrival platform. Let me know any arrangements you have been able to make. I leave myself entirely in your hands, and soon in your arms. Bye, bye, darling, sweetheart.

See you soon xxxxx Helen.

## Living in Plymouth

When Stan got his promotion to lieutenant and was posted to the Devonport Naval Base, Nellie moved to Plymouth, taking me with her. The town was being heavily bombed at the time. I must have been the only child evacuated into the bombing rather than the reverse. We lived in digs at No. 1 Townsend Villas, Mannamead, and I went to the local school at the bottom of the bank with my friend Tony Diver, who lived at No. 8. I remember Nellie taking me out of bed and wrapping me in a blanket before going down the road to the communal air-raid shelter in the school yard. I could hear the anti-aircraft fire and see the planes, but as a small boy I knew nothing of what was going on and thought it a great adventure. When we went into Plymouth town centre I was told that, if I got separated from my parents, I was to catch the tram to Crown Hill and get off at our stop. Returning to the city years later, I failed to go straight to our old home in Townsend Villas because I went to Crown Hill instead.

While Stan was good at giving financial advice to others, he was never as good at managing his own money and ran an overdraft for most of his life. In 1944 Stan was taken to court by Ridings Stores of Manchester for arrears of £9 12s for a Portadyne radio receiver he had hired from them in 1941, and for which he had failed to pay the rental. The hire fee was 2s 3d a week for the first six months, reducing in stages to 1s 3d a week in the third year. Stan took me to Devonport, and I was very impressed to see him being saluted by all the sailors.

## Giving Birth

Nellie was living in Plymouth when her second child and first daughter Penelope was born on 2 August 1945 at a private nursing home at Devonport. The charges were £1 booking fee plus ten guineas (£10 10s) for nursing and two weeks' residence. Child allowance in 1945 was 12s 6d a week per child. It would be interesting to compare present-day practices. Nellie's instructions from the nursing home were:

Patient should bring in:

| | |
|---|---|
| 5 dozen non-soluble sanitary towels | 1 roll of cotton wool |
| Comb and brush | Soap and flannel |
| Toothbrush and paste | Nail-brush |
| Safety pins | Soft slippers |
| 3 nightdresses | Bedjacket |
| Sanitary belt | Dressing gown |
| 2 ration books (mum and baby) | Gas mask |
| Identity card | Bath towels, marked |
| Cake of soap for baby | |

Expectant mothers should take each day:

| | |
|---|---|
| 2 pints of milk | cabbage |
| 2 eggs | lettuce or spinach |
| butter | sea fish twice weekly |
| fresh fruit | liver once weekly |
| meat | |

(Don't forget to take one teaspoonful of cod liver oil twice daily to make the baby's bones and teeth strong.)

## Nellie's Jobs

*[A testimonial c. 1940]*

To whom it may concern
Previous to the outbreak of war, Miss Colleen Mape was
under my charge in the important Manchester Branch of
Tote Investors Ltd. Owing to the suspension of the
provincial business of the company, all engagements were
terminated. I have pleasure in testifying to the ability and
integrity of Miss Mape. She was always attentive to her
duties and gave the utmost satisfaction.

J. Hayes
Late Manager
Manchester Office
Tote Investors Ltd.

While Nellie was working for the Tote in Manchester as a
telephonist, her picture appeared on the front page of the
*Manchester Evening News* of 24 July 1939. There was a fire at
the building in Market Street where she worked. It was a small
fire and no one was hurt. The *MEN*'s lead story that day quoted
prime minister Neville Chamberlain as denying that there would
be any 'peace bribe' to Germany. The Second World War began
on 3 September 1939, just six weeks later. On the same front
page, Lewis's (Manchester's main department store) was
advertising 'a matching set of three' British Bemberg stockings
for 1s 8½d. 'Always one stocking in hand in case of laddering,
mislaying or losing one of a pair,' said the blurb.

To: Miss E. Mape
358 Lower Broughton Road, Salford 7
31 October 1939

> Home Office
> Air Raid Precautions
> North-western Regional Office
> Arkwright House
> Parsonage Gardens
> Manchester 3

Madam
I am directed by the Secretary of State to offer you a short-term appointment as a temporary telephonist in the Home Department upon the following terms: the appointment will date from the day on which you took up duty, i.e. 5 September 1939, and will carry salary at the rate of £2 1s 6d per week.

[etc.]

I am
Sir/Madam
Your obedient servant
J. Cramp
Establishment Officer.

The appointment was subject to the Official Secrets Act. After all, there was a war on. This particular job was terminated in March 1940. Nellie asked why and was told it was 'due to the necessity for reducing staff'. Typically, she wouldn't go quietly. On 29 June 1948, Nellie was given a provisional appointment as a clerical assistant with the Central Office of Information in Manchester, on one year's probation. Again, she worked as a telephonist. Nellie resigned from her job at the COI in

June 1950. Her third child, Rosalind, was born two months later. Nellie continued to work part-time until she won a place at Manchester University in 1969 as a mature student. She went on to gain BA and MA degrees. As well as becoming a teacher later in life, Nellie was a moderator in GCSE English for the Northern Examinations and Assessment Board until 1992, at which time she was still employed as an external examiner.

## Nellie the Hoarder

A tiny, delightful item left by my mother: 'This is a bit of hair of Nellie Mape, aged 15. 28 September 1935.' A small tuft of dark-brown hair. But why did she keep it? Nellie was a hoarder – rather like my wife Frances. After Stan died, Nellie moved away from Bury in Lancashire and went to Yorkshire to live in a bungalow near Skipton. Nellie was a super-hoarder, and clearly it was impossible to take everything from the huge, rambling Birtle Edge house and fit it into her new home. My sisters ordered a skip to aid the move. But as fast as her three daughters put items into the skip to be taken to the tip, Nellie would nip out and drag them back into the house again.

Over the years Nellie acquired hundreds of books, and she spent several more years cataloguing them on record cards which she painstakingly typed out. She was notorious for going into second-hand bookshops with a plastic sack and hauling away the contents. For all that, Nellie advertised 'books and bric-a-brac' for sale at the Bolton & District Collectors Flea-market & Autojumble in November 1973.

Stan died in 1993, aged eighty-one. His non-religious funeral was held at Rochdale Crematorium. The music played included 'Lullaby of Birdland' by pianist George Shearing, and Ella Fitzgerald singing 'Lady Be Good' and 'Blue Moon'. There were readings from Shelley and Keats.

Nellie died in 2001, also aged eighty-one. Her funeral was held in Skipton in North Yorkshire, where she had moved after Stan's death. Of Nellie's surviving siblings, only her sister Nora was able to attend, in a wheelchair, along with her two daughters, our cousins Maureen and Bernadette. As at Stan's funeral, all Nellie's four children were there, along with friends and other family members. As with Stan, it was a non-religious occasion. The music played was a Bach harpsichord concerto, the *Coronation Street* theme, and 'Abide with Me' sung by a Welsh male-voice choir. We also played two unique recordings of Nellie and Stan singing together. They recorded the songs 'Not Like Other Girls' and 'If I Were a Lad' (both written by Stan) in 1938, and 'Not Like Other Girls' again and 'Little Yellow Basket' in 1992. I shall always be grateful to my brother-in-law, Geoffrey Durham, for putting these recordings on CD for us.

It was 4.30 p.m. on Boxing Day, 26 December 1937 when Nellie and Stan met for the first time. He was playing the piano, the tune 'I Want to Be Happy'. Nellie never forgot, and she did make Stan happy for the rest of his life.

# Notes

## Chapter 1

1. The Irish came to Liverpool and Manchester in large numbers following the potato famine of 1846, and a further blight in 1879. Following the 1870 Education Act, a Catholic mission was set up in the Bradford area of Manchester and a school built in Willow Street. The mission became the parish of St Brigid's in 1879, named after St Brigid of Kildare. The Catholic girls' school between Butterworth Street and Howarth Street was opened in 1893. A third school was built on the corner of Cross Street and Queen Street in 1929. The first Catholic church was a former Anglican one from Atherton eleven miles away, dismantled and re-erected by the men of the parish. It was replaced by a fine stone building in 1901. At that time there were 5,000 Catholics in the parish with 1,000 children of school age. The parish priest in Nellie's time was Fr Joseph Fitzgerald, born in Limerick, who came to St Brigid's in 1922. Known to his fellow clergy as 'Big Mick', Fr Fitzgerald remained in charge of the parish for forty-two years until his death in 1964 at the age of ninety (*St Brigid's Centenary History*, Harry Montgomery, 1979).

2. Manchester City Libraries, local image collection M155628.

3. Jack Mape's disability. I always understood that my grandfather, who died when I was only three months old, had suffered from wounds sustained in the First World War, which had been aggravated by gas. He was often in a convalescent home for skin grafts, which were usually unsuccessful. My aunties tell me that their father often had to lie on the sofa at home, and he was in such pain at times that he could only bear his daughter Winnie to tend the weeping wound in his back. Jack suffered from the cold, and he set fire to himself while standing warming himself with his back to the kitchen range fire. He rolled himself up in a carpet to put out the flames, but suffered burns which led at least indirectly to his death. I was Jack's first grandchild. Despite the earlier rift with her father, Nellie took me to see him in hospital when I was just a few weeks old. He died soon afterwards.

4. St Mary's Church in Mulberry Street.

5. The doubling room was where two single threads of cotton were spun together, producing what was still a fine but much stronger thread. It is likely that most of the production was for export.
6. Unfortunately, we have no record of these.

## Chapter 2

1. As few houses had bathrooms, the Manchester City Corporation provided public 'slipper baths' where people could wash and have a bath. Some were quite elaborate, incorporating Turkish and steam baths. Some were attached to swimming pools. There were also municipal wash-houses. The term 'slipper baths' comes from the use of slippers to avoid spreading foot infections. The Bradford district swimming pool was one of twenty-four in Manchester, and was quite near Nellie's home. It cost 1s 6d for a swim, in contrast to the 'posh' pools at Victoria in the city centre and in the genteel suburb of Chorlton-cum-Hardy (where Stan lived), where 2s 6d a time was charged to keep out the riff-raff. School-children and the unemployed could swim free under certain circumstances: 'Scholars over the age of seven years are admitted free to the second-class swimming baths, and are provided with towels and bathing drawers, any weekday except Saturday, in the charge of a teacher or master' (Manchester Corporation annual report, 1934); unemployed men were allowed free use of the second-class swimming and washing baths. Bradford swimming baths also included a wash-house, one of nineteen in the city. It was situated in Bank Street, next to Manchester United's old ground.
2. I have no information about the 'letter to mother' game; the usual form of street lighting in those days was by gas lamps, each on a metal lamp standard which had a convenient arm just below the lantern for the gasman to rest his ladder against. This was ideal for tying a rope to.
3. In 1845 Engels noted that there was already a trend for women to go to work, leaving their husbands to look after the house and family. 'Factory hands: the wife supports the family, the husband sits at home, tends the children, sweeps the room and cooks. This case happens very frequently; in Manchester alone, many hundred such men could be cited, condemned to domestic occupations' ('Single Branches of Industry', *The Condition of the Working Class in England*, Friedrich Engels, 1845).
4. Local cinemas included the New Royal on Ashton New Road, the Don in Beswick, and the Osborne at Miles Platting. As a teenager, Nellie records that she watched films at these Manchester cinemas: Hippodrome, Shaftesbury, Grand, Queen's, Rivoli, King's, Corona, Ardwick, Fair,

Olympia. She went to the Metropole Theatre, danced at the Victoria Hotel, and attended meetings and other events at the Wesley Hall and the Free Trade Hall.

5.  Naphtha is 'a volatile bituminous liquid, of a strong peculiar odour and very inflammable'. It was used to light lamps, but was not suitable for indoor use.

6.  Quassia Chips are still used in pot pourri. Their main use in Nellie's day was to get rid of head lice.

7.  Camphor is a strong-smelling oil extracted from trees in the Far East. It was used in insecticides and in making mothballs.

## Chapter 3

1.  'Gathering Peascods' – a traditional English country dance, recorded in The English Dance Master, 1651.

2.  Angela Brazil wrote about middle-class English schoolgirls having adventures. Her books were enormously popular from the 1900s to the 1950s. She wrote forty-eight 'school' novels, starting with *The Fortunes of Philippa* in 1906. Angela Brazil died in 1947, still writing.

3.  Miss Catherine O'Reilly, who became head in 1923, introduced school uniforms for the Whit Walks, allowing the parents to pay weekly for the clothes which were bought in bulk from wholesalers in Manchester. Weeks before the actual walks, Miss O'Reilly would practise marching with the girls in the school yard and then in the surrounding streets, the headmistress beating time on a biscuit tin. Not only were they neatly dressed, the girls were always praised for the military smartness of their walking. Miss O'Reilly also started to make use of the stage on the upper floor of the girls' school, presenting very successful and colourful variety shows and revues. Practically every girl who went through the school during the 1930s appeared in one or other of her productions. She was ably abetted by her staff and encouraged by one of the assistant priests, Fr Thomas Hourigan, who served in the parish from 1930 to 1936 (*St Brigid's Centenary History*, Harry Montgomery 1979).

4.  The English Steel Corporation's massive North Street Works, just across Ashton New Road. Nellie kept two of her work record cards, headed 'ESC Ltd, small tools dept, cutter section'.

## Chapter 4

1.  *Peg's Paper* was a magazine for women and girls, popular between the wars.

2. Nellie's father Jack Mape was secretary/treasurer of the St Brigid's football team, who won the Manchester & District Catholic League (Hamill Cup) and the Cassidy Cup in successive seasons, 1931/2 and 1932/3. The Bradford district has a strong connection with top soccer club Manchester United, who moved there from their original North Road ground in nearby Newton Heath in 1893. The players used to change at the Queen's Hotel in Ashton New Road before walking to their then home ground at Bank Street, next to the power station which overlooked Nellie's home. When Man United won the FA Cup in 1909 (beating Bristol City 1–0), the hotel's name was changed to 'The United'. Man United moved to Old Trafford the following year. Manchester City moved from Maine Road to their new stadium just across the road from Gibbon Street in 2003. It is only a few hundred yards from where Man United used to play!

3. Flip, Flop, Floorbang – I have no idea what this game was.

4. A 'red rec' was a playground or recreation ground that had no grass, only a hard surface of red gravel or asphalt.

5. Two Ball and One Two Three Alaira were played either singly or in pairs, almost invariably by girls. You would bounce a tennis ball against a wall and the pavement in various ways, under and over your leg, sometimes turning to catch the ball on the bounce.

# Chapter 6

1. The first Catholic walk to Manchester was held in 1834. The Whit Friday Walk commenced at eight o'clock in the morning and usually ended in the early afternoon. The same evening, a dance would be held in the new infants' school. The sprung maple-wood floor was excellent for dancing, and was far superior to the old knotted boards of the girls' school. The following day saw the parish outing to Holywell, which started at 6 a.m. The parents were usually still half-asleep as they boarded the three coaches, but the children were always excited. Most of the children were asleep when the coaches returned at around ten o'clock in the evening, for it was an exhausting day for everyone, though one that was thoroughly enjoyed. The climax of the weekend was the Trinity Sunday walk around the parish. It was the day when the infants' school, now under the headship of Miss Teresa Johnson, who had succeeded Miss Rabbit in 1934, joined the procession. There were over 1,000 children in the three schools, a figure which when added to those walking with the men's and women's confraternities, the Children of Mary and the Guild of St Agnes, three banners and two bands, provided an

impressive demonstration of the faith. The traditional Manchester Catholic Whit Friday Walks ceased in 1974, replaced by a much smaller procession in the centre of Manchester (*St Brigid's Centenary History*, Harry Montgomery, 1979).

## Chapter 7

1.  When I was ten or eleven, my mother very proudly showed me this essay, which she kept in a bound volume at home.
2.  At other times, the Rechabites recorded her as 'Sister Nellie Mape'. When Nellie was born, she was registered as 'Ellen Mape', but was later given the names Helen Colleen. On her marriage certificate she is styled as 'Ellen, otherwise Helen Colleen Mape'. To our cousins, she was 'Auntie Nellie'. To her family, and at school, she was 'Nellie'. So 'Nellie' it is.
3.  *Juvenile Rechabite* magazine, August 1935.
4.  I think Nellie meant actually getting published. She had been writing at least since her early days with Stan, and it was 1951 when she wrote the first draft of 'Empire Street'.

## Chapter 8

1.  Blanco is the cream you used to wipe onto your white tennis shoes or pumps to get them pure and gleaming. Somehow, I don't think today's generation bother with blanco when their designer trainers are scuffed – they just get a new pair.
2.  Years later, I had a holiday job working in this same Lyons teashop.

## Chapter 9

1.  Mrs Smith is not shown on the register for Gibbon Street. I assume she lived in one of the several side streets.
2.  Barnshaw's grocer's shop. Stan Wood used the name 'Barnshaw' as a character in some of his fictional writings.
3.  Donkey stones, etc. were used to 'stone', or decorate, front doorsteps and window sills. They were solid blocks in different colours which became a paste when dampened and rubbed on the flags or stones.
4.  Monday was washday, which usually started early in the morning when pans of water were boiled over the coal fire and then poured into the washtub. In a kitchen full of steam, the clothes were scrubbed on a ribbed wood or metal washboard and pounded with a posser. After

rinsing, the water was then squeezed from the clothes by running them through a mangle or wringing machine before they were finally hung out to dry in the backyard. They were pressed normally by two flat irons heated alternately by the open fire.

The homes were dusted and tidied every day, but Friday was generally regarded as cleaning day by the female members of the family. Again it started in the early morning. The living-room fire was not lit until later in the day so as to allow the iron framework of the fireplace to be black-leaded. It was then polished until it gleamed. The house was cleaned thoroughly room by room and, finally, the steps and window sills were brown- or cream-stoned.

Friday night was the children's bath night. The zinc bathtub was placed before the fire and filled and refilled with hot water, depending on the number of children to be bathed. Particular attention was always paid to the children's hair for fear of head lice. The hair was always washed separately, and then combed with a fine-tooth comb until the scalp was sore. Before the introduction of Derbac soap and other proprietary remedies, the simplest way of getting rid of the lice was to soak the hair well with a mixture of kerosene oil and olive oil in equal parts. The hair was then covered with a cap which was worn overnight, and the oil washed off next morning with soap and warm water. This was repeated for two or three successive days (*St Brigid's Centenary History*, Harry Montgomery, 1979).

My mother was still using a mangle (hand-wringer) with wooden rollers and washboard when I was a teenager. I had to operate the mangle, but I borrowed the washboard for other purposes. It was the first musical instrument I played in the amateur skiffle and folk groups I belonged to during the mid-1950s, before graduating to banjo and guitar. I later played in various semi-professional rock-and-roll, dance and jazz bands.

5. 'Stoning' of flags, steps and window sills, particularly the front doorstep to the house, is a dying tradition that still clings on in some northern towns. Nowadays it is usually confined to a coloured strip around the edge of the step. In Lancashire, as Nellie describes, the preferred colours were beige, brown and white. In the North-east and Yorkshire, a deep red with black edging was popular.

# Chapter 10

1. In 1965, Manchester Corporation issued compulsory purchase orders prior to demolishing large parts of the Bradford area, reducing the

population of St Brigid's parish from 3,000 to 600. In the summer of 1966 demolition companies with their cranes and bulldozers started to flatten the area, leaving St Brigid's Church and schools in isolation. The occupants of the old houses were scattered to the four corners of Manchester. With them went the years of neighbourliness, friendship and the spirit of community. It was the end of an era. Earlier, in the hope of retaining the people as part of the community, particularly the aged, an action group was formed. Efforts were made to persuade Manchester's housing officials to allow those who wished to stay in the area to remain in their homes until the new Wimpey estate was completed on what had been the area surrounding Parker Street. The men of the parish visited every house, asking those who wanted to stay to sign a petition that would eventually be presented to the Lord Mayor. Councillors attended packed meetings in the girls' school and, as a result of the petition, a meeting was arranged between the action committee, led by MP Charles Morris, and corporation housing officials. It soon became apparent that the officials were not prepared to alter their reconstruction schedules. The heart had been torn from the parish. (*St Brigid's Centenary History*, Harry Montgomery, 1979.)

2.   In 1957, the Medical Officer of Health commented, 'The Ruhr in Germany used to have the highest fall of soot in the world. This distinction now belongs to an area covering Miles Platting, Bradford and Beswick.' It was the grimiest, most densely populated and most built-up area of Manchester. The *City and Suburban News* wrote, 'Its trademark is an obnoxious smell which pervades the area and haunts its long-suffering residents by day and night.' The area almost had its own microclimate due to steam condensing and falling like rain. (Manchester City Libraries.)

## Chapter 11

1.   Written under Stan Wood's pen name, Ross Graham, *Death on a Smoke Boat*, described as 'a story of espionage at sea', was published in January 1947 by Hurst & Blackett, a hardback retailing at 9s 6d. Stan told me his book should have been published immediately after the war, but this was delayed due to a paper shortage.

2.   ESC (English Steel Corporation) was the engineering firm where Nellie started work as a progress chaser just after her fourteenth birthday. It occupied a huge site just south of Ashton New Road and close to Gibbon Street.